The Pennsylvania Interstate Banking and Thrift Legislation
and Its Impact on Financial Institutions

By THE FINANCIAL INSTITUTIONS GROUP OF STEVENS & LEE

PACKARD PRESS

FINANCIAL PUBLICATIONS DIVISION

10th & Spring Garden Streets
Philadelphia, PA 19123
1-800-722-2447
1-800-722-7800 in PA

First Edition   June 1987

Copyright© 1987 by Packard Press.

All rights reserved. No part of this publication may be reproduced, stored in a retrieval system, or transmitted, in any form or by any means, electronic, mechanical, photocopying, recording, or otherwise, without the prior written permission of the author and publisher.

This publication is designed to provide accurate and authoritative information in regard to the subject matter covered. It is sold with the understanding that the publisher is not engaged in rendering legal, accounting, or other professional service. If legal advice or other expert assistance is required, the services of a professional should be sought.

Printed in the United States of America.
ISBN 0936093595

Publisher's Note

Packard Press, one of the nation's leading financial printers, is pleased to furnish you with this informative compendium enabling you to better comprehend and interpret the Pennsylvania Interstate Banking and Thrift Legislation, its impact and the new opportunities presented by this legislation.

Working closely with the financial institutions group of Stevens & Lee and Ryan, Beck & Co., we have published a volume which is both comprehensive and timely. The work contains Delaware's and New Jersey's recent passage of similar legislation.

The book will give you insight into the new arena which the Pennsylvania General Assembly created, when it passed Senate bills 1075, 1389 and 1390. The authors address the commercial bank and thrift legislation, the FHLBB interstate regulation as well as the interstate ramifications of the legislation on the states located within the compact.

Many diverse technical applications were coordinated to make this book possible — a comprehensive range of electronic printing services, including computerized typesetting, facsimile delivery, electronic data transmission, laser printing techniques and more. Careful, effective utilization of these modern resources enables Packard Press to deliver on time, every time, and at a competitive price.

These modern technological systems, combined with the strategic input of experienced Packard Press professionals, can help satisfy your informational needs as well. We are expertly staffed to handle all your financial printing requirements from the preparation of complex registration documents, official statements and documents of international fiance, to the complete design and printing of annual reports, interim reports and proxy material.

In addition, our knowledgeable Packard Press account executives will give you all the personal attention necessary to satisy your particular printing needs, then follow through on all job details — from the receipt of manuscript (copy, diskette, magnetic tape or direct transmission) to the timely delivery or electronic transmission of the appropriate documents to the Securities and Exchange Commission, rating agencies, underwriters or shareholders.

The Packard Press
Frank E. Scullin
Senior Vice President

Please refer to the inside back cover of this book for a complete list of all the financial reference books published by Packard Press.

PREFACE

This article was prepared by the financial institutions group of the law firm of Stevens & Lee, Reading and Valley Forge, Pennsylvania in cooperation with Packard Press. The article is intended to outline Pennsylvania's interstate bank and thrift legislation in an organized format and provide insight into the effect of the legislation on Pennsylvania's banks and thrifts. It is designed for use principally by bank and thrift officers and directors, as well as the professionals involved in bank and thrift mergers and acquisitions in Pennsylvania and in the states located in the interstate banking and thrift region defined by the Pennsylvania statutes. The article is in keeping with the commitment of both Packard Press and Stevens & Lee to financial institutions in Pennsylvania.

Both Packard Press and Stevens & Lee wish to acknowledge the editorial assistance which they received from Ryan, Beck & Co., investment bankers and bank and thrift consultants, as well as a number of bank and thrift executives throughout Pennsylvania.

TABLE OF CONTENTS

Page
Number

Executive Summary 1
I. Introduction 6
II. The Pennsylvania Commercial Bank Legislation 7
   A. The Existing Federal Legislative Scheme 7
   B. Pennsylvania's Pre-existing Legislation 7
   C. The New Legislation 8
      1. The Five Requirements
         a. The Regional Compact for Commercial Banks and Bank Holding Companies
         b. Reciprocity for Bank Holding Companies
         c. Department of Banking Approval
            (1) The Application and Department of Banking Jurisdiction
            (2) Scope of Review
            (3) Review of Credit Practices
            (4) Review of Basic Transaction Account Services
         d. Subsidiary Limitation
   D. Interstate Expansion Under the New Legislation 17
III. The Thrift Legislation 19
   A. The Existing Federal Legislative Scheme 19
   B. Pennsylvania's Pre-existing Legislation 19
   C. The New Legislation 20
      1. The Three Requirements
         a. The Regional Compact for Thrifts
         b. Reciprocity for Thrifts
         c. Department of Banking Approval
   D. The Effect of the SLHCA 24
   E. Other Differences Between the Commercial Bank and Thrift Legislation 25
IV. The FHLBB's Interstate Regulation 26
      1. Basic Authority
      2. Basic Interstate Rules
      3. Interstate Expansion in Supervisory Cases
      4. Interstate Rights for Thrifts under Pennsylvania and Federal Laws
V. The Legislation of Other States in the Region 33
VI. Impact of Interstate Legislation 37
   A. The Effect on Competition 38
      1. Regional Effects
      2. National Effects
      3. Local Effects
   B. The Effect on Deposit Flows 42
   C. The Regional Market Focus 44
   D. The Regional Landscape 45
   E. Criteria for Determining Strategy 47
   F. Goals and Strategies 50

Page Number

VII. Conclusion 55
VIII. The Legislation
    A. Exhibit "A"; Senate Bill No. 1075 56
    B. Exhibit "B"; Senate Bill No. 1389 64
    C. Exhibit "C"; Senate Bill No. 1390 74
    D. Exhibit "D"; FHLBB Interstate Branching Regulation .. 82
    E. Exhibit "E"; McFadden Act 91
    F. Exhibit "F"; Douglas Amendment 94
    G. Exhibit "G"; Department of Banking Applications 95
    H. Exhibit "H"; Savings and Loan Holding Company Act . 105

EXECUTIVE SUMMARY

THE PENNSYLVANIA INTERSTATE BANKING AND THRIFT LEGISLATION AND ITS IMPACT ON PENNSYLVANIA FINANCIAL INSTITUTIONS

The Pennsylvania General Assembly has passed Senate Bills 1075, 1389 and 1390. The three Senate Bills permit the interstate expansion of commercial banks, savings banks and savings associations, respectively. When coupled with the existing federal legislative scheme regulating bank holding companies and the adoption by the Federal Home Loan Bank Board (the "FHLBB") of a revised interstate regulation for federal thrifts, the result will be a new and exciting era for the financial services industry in Pennsylvania. This article discusses these legislative initiatives and the FHLBB regulation in detail. A short synopsis of this article follows.

The Commercial Bank Legislation.

- Under existing federal law, national banks cannot expand interstate, and bank holding companies can do so only to the extent that the laws of the state the holding company wishes to enter expressly permits such entry. Accordingly, the passage of legislation at the state level permitting interstate banking is the essential element necessary to permit interstate expansion of bank holding companies.

- Prior to enactment of Senate Bill 1075 banks located in Pennsylvania could (i) not expand interstate, and (ii) branch only into bicontiguous counties and the counties of Allegheny, Delaware, Montgomery and Philadelphia. Pennsylvania bank holding companies could not (i) expand interstate, and (ii) prior to 1990, acquire more than eight banking subsidiaries.

- Under Senate Bill 1075 a bank holding company (but not a bank) located outside Pennsylvania can enter Pennsylvania if:

    — the holding company is located in Delaware, Kentucky, Maryland, New Jersey, Ohio, Virginia, West Virginia or the District of Columbia;

    — 75% of the deposits of the acquiror are located in the foregoing states and Pennsylvania;

    — the laws of the home state of the acquiror are "reciprocal" as determined by the Pennsylvania Department of Banking — i.e. such laws permit entry by Pennsylvania bank holding companies;

    — the acquisition does not violate the eight banking subsidiary limit; and

    — the Pennsylvania Department of Banking ("DOB") approves the acquisition.

- The requirement that the bank holding company be located in the region and that 75% of the deposits of the holding company be located within the region expires after March 4, 1990, thus opening Pennsylvania to nationwide banking. Violation of these provisions prior to their expiration requires divestiture.

- The laws of another state are reciprocal if such laws allow Pennsylvania bank holding companies to acquire bank or bank holding companies in that state on terms and conditions substantially no more restrictive than those applicable to an intrastate acquisition.
- The DOB has broad jurisdiction to review any interstate transaction. With respect to acquisitions of out-of-state entities by Pennsylvania entities, the review consists of a determination by the DOB that the acquiror will meet certain credit and transaction account needs of Pennsylvania businesses and residents. With respect to the acquisition of a Pennsylvania entity by an out-of-state bank holding company, the review includes the foregoing plus an analysis of (i) the financial and managerial resources of the applicant, (ii) the financial history and future prospects of the applicant and the Pennsylvania acquiree, (iii) the resulting concentration of resources, and (iv) the convenience and needs of the public.
- In theory interstate expansion could be accomplished through branching, merger (i.e., two entities statutorily merge resulting in one survivor or a new entity) or acquisition (i.e., acquiror acquires all the stock of the acquiree and operates it as a subsidiary, the acquiror thus being or becoming a holding company). As a result of the existing federal legislation and the new Pennsylvania bill, the following chart describes the permissible interstate rights of Pennsylvania banking organizations:

	Branching	Merger	Acquisition
National Bank located in Pennsylvania	No	No	No
Pennsylvania State Bank	No	No	No
Operating Bank Subsidiary of Pennsylvania Bank Holding Company (i.e. not an interim bank)	No	No	No
Pennsylvania Bank Holding Company	N/A	Yes (with bank holding company only)	Yes (tender or exchange offer or other purchase of the stock or assets of a bank or bank holding company; merger of target into interim bank subsidiary)

The Thrift Legislation

- Until the FHLBB amended its branching regulation in April 1986, federal thrifts could not expand interstate. In addition, under the Savings and Loan Holding Company Act ("SLHCA") savings and loan holding companies cannot control FSLIC or FDIC-insured thrifts in more than one state.
- Similarly, under Pennsylvania law, savings banks, savings associations and holding companies could not expand interstate.

- Senate Bills 1389 and 1390 permit savings banks, savings and loans and savings and loan holding companies to enter Pennsylvania if:
  - the entrant is located in the same eight state region described in the commercial banking bill;
  - the law of the home state of the entrant is reciprocal; and
  - the DOB approves the entry.
- The thrift legislation contains no date upon which the regional requirement will expire. Therefore, full nationwide expansion of thrifts into Pennsylvania will not occur absent further legislative action.
- The law of the home state of the entrant is reciprocal if (i) a Pennsylvania thrift can acquire a thrift in that state on terms and conditions not substantially more onerous than those imposed on *intrastate* acquisitions, *and* (ii) a Pennsylvania thrift can acquire a thrift in that state on terms and conditions reasonably equivalent to acquisitions of a Pennsylvania thrift by a thrift from that state.
- The DOB approval process requires a review of the credit and basic transaction services provided by the acquiror.
- The commercial banking bill only permits bank holding companies to expand interstate while the thrift bills allow thrifts and holding companies to do so. But, because the SLHCA does not permit the existence of thrift holding companies which control thrifts in more than one state (except in supervisory cases), as a practical matter only thrifts, and not thrift holding companies, possess interstate rights.

The FHLBB's Interstate Regulation

- The FHLBB promulgated a regulation in April 1986 which permits a federal thrift, subject to the SLHCA, to expand interstate if the law of the home state of the thrift *and* the law of the state it seeks to enter would permit the transaction if the thrift were state-chartered. Therefore, Pennsylvania's new thrift legislation partially enables federal thrifts located in Pennsylvania to expand interstate.
- The basic authority to expand is determined by federal law but the regulation specifies that no state approvals are required. Nevertheless, Pennsylvania's legislation does require DOB approval of interstate transactions involving federal thrifts.
- The regulation establishes certain interstate expansion rules the net result of which is to permit only one federal thrift within a holding company structure to expand interstate. This may encourage conversion of federal thrifts to state charters.
- The FHLBB regulation also permits thrifts which acquire a failed or failing thrift to expand interstate into the greater of (i) three additional designated states, or (ii) all the states into which the acquiree could expand by reason of regional legislation. Preference is given to geographically contiguous expansion.
- As a result of the passage of Pennsylvania's interstate thrift bills, the adoption of the FHLBB interstate regulation and the constraints of the SLHCA, the following chart describes the interstate rights of thrift organizations (stock or mutual):

	Permissible Activity		
	Branching	Merger	Acquisition
State Thrift	Yes	Yes	No
Federal Thrift	Yes	Yes	No
Thrift Holding Company that is an insured institution	Yes	Yes	No
Thrift Subsidiary of Thrift Holding Company	Yes	Yes	No
Thrift Holding Company (not an insured institution)	N/A	No	No

The Legislation of Other States in the Region

- Delaware, Kentucky, Maryland, New Jersey, Ohio and West Virginia have enacted interstate banking legislation which is or with the passage of time will be reciprocal with Pennsylvania's statute. Virginia and the District of Columbia have nonreciprocal legislation. A small number of interstate acquisitions have been announced, the latest being the recently-announced acquisition of Delaware Trust Company by Meridian Bancorp, Inc.
- Maryland, New Jersey, Ohio and West Virginia have enacted interstate thrift legislation which is, or will be, reciprocal with Pennsylvania's legislation. Delaware has enacted interstate legislation affecting savings banks. Virginia has enacted nonreciprocal interstate thrift legislation and District of Columbia thrifts are governed by the FHLBB's interstate regulation. Kentucky has no interstate thrift legislation.

The Impact of Interstate Legislation

- Although consolidation will probably occur on a regional and eventually national level, an oligopoly is not the inevitable result.
- The financial services industry is already an effective geographic intermediary for the flow of funds with smaller banks actually more likely than larger banks to cause a geographic redistribution of funds through investment in nonloan assets. Therefore, the removal of interstate barriers should not, in and of itself, cause any geographic shift in deposit flows.
- Larger banks and thrifts may be compelled by competitive forces to adjust their market focus from a relatively local focus to a larger regional focus.
- As a result of consolidation, the banking industry in the region may be dominated, in terms of both loan volume, and to a lesser extent, deposit volume, by eight to twelve holding companies. Because no intrastate consolidation for thrifts has occurred, a similar assessment is not yet possible for thrifts.
- Despite the regional dominance of large institutions, community institutions, efficient institutions with a stable, low cost of funds and those which serve a particular market niche will survive.

- Each financial institution must evaluate itself to determine its place in the regional landscape. The criteria which will be determinative are:
  - capital adequacy;
  - market capitalization;
  - managerial depth;
  - franchise area (especially attractive are institutions that are located near state borders); and
  - asset size.

The most important of these five elements is probably market capitalization because today the "currency" of merger and acquisition transactions is the acquiror's stock.

- In the banking industry, Pennsylvania, because of its central location and its numerous, large institutions, will probably be a net acquiring state. With respect to thrifts, whether Pennsylvania will be a net acquiror is not yet clear.

- Bank holding companies with assets in excess of $8 to $10 billion or more can aspire to a regional role. Other slightly smaller institutions can similarly aspire, but with greater difficulty.

- Other banking institutions of moderate size can grow with or without acquisitions and can sell at a premium, enter into stakeout agreements, or maintain independence, as they choose.

- Small, weak banks should consider taking the steps now which are necessary to prevent further decline *and* maintain independence, possibly through the use of alternative structures such as franchising. Such institutions may also consider selling before the optimal size of acquisition targets exceeds their asset size. Small, stronger institutions can sell, enter into stakeout agreements, or maintain their independence as they choose.

- Thrifts with asset size in excess of $500 million can reasonably seek a regional role because so little consolidation has occurred in the thrift industry and because merger conversion transactions with mutual thrifts entail the addition of capital rather than the expenditure of capital.

- Small stock thrifts are attractive acquisition candidates but they also can grow readily through acquisition and achieve a larger regional role.

- With due regard to regulatory capital considerations, mutual thrifts can merge among themselves, convert to stock ownership and expand their possibilities or enter into a merger conversion transaction.

- Because it is a recent trend and because empirical data is not yet available, the authors have not attempted to assess the impact that the erosion of barriers in the international financial and capital markets and the ascendancy of foreign financial institutions will have on the composition of the domestic financial institutions industry.

THE PENNSYLVANIA INTERSTATE BANKING AND THRIFT LEGISLATION AND ITS IMPACT ON PENNSYLVANIA FINANCIAL INSTITUTIONS

I. INTRODUCTION

Pennsylvania has entered a new era in the financial services industry. The Pennsylvania legislature passed, and Governor Thornburgh signed, interstate banking legislation for Pennsylvania based commercial banks,[1] savings banks[2] and savings and loan associations.[3] Shortly before adoption of this legislation, the Federal Home Loan Bank Board adopted a new regulation which permits interstate expansion by federal thrifts if the laws of the home state of the federal thrift and the state that the institution desires to enter would permit it.[4] As a result of the passage of legislation at the state level and the existence of complementary federal laws and regulations, the financial services industry may well undergo rapid and sweeping change.[5]

The purpose of this article is to summarize and analyze Pennsylvania's legislation and the FHLBB's regulation and assess the impact of these important legislative and regulatory changes on both large and small institutions and on intrastate and interstate merger and acquisition activity. In addition, although similar in most respects, Pennsylvania's legislation for commercial banks does contain some important differences from the thrift legislation and this article will highlight the differences among the bills. Finally, this article will express the views of the authors on the likely future composition of the financial services industry in Pennsylvania.[6]

---

1. The commercial bank legislation, Senate Bill 1075, amends the Pennsylvania Banking Code of 1965. The complete text of this legislation is set forth in Exhibit "A."
2. The bills for savings banks is Senate Bill 1389 which also amends the Pennsylvania Banking Code of 1965. The relevant text from this bill is set forth in Exhibit "B."
3. The bill for savings and loan associations is Senate Bill 1390 which amends the Savings Association Code of 1967. The complete text of the bill is set forth in Exhibit "C."
4. 12 C.F.R. § 556.5 (originally published at 51 Fed.Reg. 16501). The complete text of this regulation and the FHLBB's accompanying commentary is set forth in Exhibit "D."
5. See Section VI *infra*.
6. Before commencing the discussion of the new legislation, a word about some of the terms used in the article is necessary. Combinations between financial institutions can occur in a variety of ways. Stock can be acquired for cash and/or the stock or securities of the acquiror. Alternatively, although not common, assets can be purchased for cash or securities and liabilities assumed. Furthermore, a combination may occur as the result of a statutory merger between the acquiror (or a subsidiary of the acquiror) and the target in exchange for cash or securities of the acquiror. In general, the Pennsylvania legislation and the legislation of other states appear to use the generic terms "acquisition" or "acquire" to describe all these transactions in which an interstate combination is effected. Unless the context otherwise requires, these terms will be used in this article in the same manner. However, in Sections II, III and IV it is sometimes necessary to distinguish between the types of structures utilized to effect interstate transactions. In those cases, the term "branching" will be used to connote *de novo* establishment of a branch or the purchase of the assets of a branch and the assumption of the branch's liabilities. The term "merger" will be used to describe a transaction in which an acquiror (or a subsidiary of the acquiror) and the target engage in a merger in which one entity survives or the two combining entities form one new entity. Finally, the term "acquisition" will be used, in this context, to describe a transaction in which the acquiror acquires all the stock of the acquiree and operates it as an independent subsidiary. As a result of this last type of transaction, the acquiror becomes a holding company (if it is not already one) and becomes subject to

II. THE PENNSYLVANIA COMMERCIAL BANK LEGISLATION

A. The Existing Federal Legislative Scheme.

Existing federal legislation governs interstate expansion of national banks and bank holding companies. The McFadden Act[7] provides that (i) a national bank may branch within the state in which it is located to the same extent that state-chartered banks may branch, and (ii) a national bank may not branch outside the state in which it is located. Other federal statutory provisions prohibit the consolidation or merger of a national bank with a national or state-chartered bank located in a different state.[8]

The ability of bank holding companies to make interstate acquisitions is governed by the Douglas Amendment to the Bank Holding Company Act of 1956 (the "BHCA").[9] The Douglas amendment provides that the Federal Reserve Board will not approve any application by a bank holding company[10] to acquire any shares of, interest in, or all or substantially all of the assets of any bank located outside the state in which the operations of the holding company's subsidiaries are conducted unless the acquisition is specifically authorized by the laws of the acquiree's home state. Until recently all state statutes prohibited such acquisitions and therefore these state statutes, when applied in concert with the Douglas Amendment, have been the major obstacle to interstate expansion.

B. Pennsylvania's Pre-existing Legislation.

Prior to the enactment of Pennsylvania Senate Bill 1075, no bank holding company, except a Pennsylvania bank holding company,[11] could acquire a national bank located in Pennsylvania, a Pennsylvania state bank,[12] or a Pennsylvania bank holding company. Furthermore, before 1986 a Pennsylvania bank holding company could only own four banking subsidiaries located in Pennsylvania and, until 1990, such holding companies can only own eight banking subsidiaries located in Pennsylvania. Thereafter, the limitation on the number of banking subsidiaries located in Pennsylvania which a Pennsylvania bank holding company can own expires. Senate Bill 1075 only eliminates the prohibition against acquisition of national banks located in Pennsylvania, Pennsylvania state banks or Pennsylvania bank holding companies by out-of-state bank holding companies. It does not alter the limit on the number of banks located in Pennsylvania which a Pennsylvania or out-of-state bank holding company can own.

---

regulation under either the Bank Holding Company Act of 1956 or the Savings and Loan Holding Company Act.
7. 12 U.S.C. § 36. The complete text of the McFadden Act is set forth in Exhibit "E."
8. 12 U.S.C. §§ 215, 215a and 215b.
9. 12 U.S.C. § 1842(d). The complete text of the Douglas Amendment is set forth in Exhibit "F."
10. The BHCA defines a bank holding company as any company which has control over any bank or any company that becomes a bank holding company. 12 U.S.C. §1841(a)(1). "Bank" as used in the statute includes both national and state banks and therefore the BHCA controls the acquisition of both national and state banks.
11. A Pennsylvania bank holding company was defined under pre-existing law, and is defined under the new law, as a holding company whose banking subsidiaries conduct their operations principally in Pennsylvania as determined by deposit concentration.
12. 7 P.S. § 115.

Under existing law, Pennsylvania state-chartered banks cannot branch,[13] merge[14] or make acquisitions[15] across state lines. With respect to branching, until 1990 Pennsylvania banks are permitted to branch only into counties of the first class, second class or second class A[16] or counties contiguous or bicontiguous to the county in which the bank has its principal place of business.[17] After 1990, full statewide branching is permitted. The passage of Senate Bill 1075 does not alter these provisions in any way.

C. The New Legislation.

Senate Bill 1075 provides that, if five conditions are met, a bank holding company[18] located outside Pennsylvania can acquire control[19] or five percent[20] or more of the voting stock of a Pennsylvania bank holding company,[21] a Pennsylvania state-chartered bank or bank and trust company or a national bank whose principal place of business is located in Pennsylvania. These five conditions are:

(i) the acquiror (a holding company) and any holding company that controls[22] it must be located in Delaware, Kentucky, Maryland, New Jersey, Ohio, Virginia, West Virginia or the District of Columbia;[23]

(ii) 75% of the deposits of the acquiror must be located within one or more of these foregoing states and Pennsylvania;

(iii) the laws of the state in which the acquiror is located (and the laws of the home state of any entity that controls the acquiror) must allow Pennsylvania bank holding companies to enter that state;

(iv) the acquisition must not violate Pennsylvania's limit on the number of subsidiaries located in Pennsylvania that a bank holding company can own; and

(v) the Pennsylvania Department of Banking (the "DOB") must approve the acquisition.

---

13. 7 P.S. § 904.
14. 7 P.S. § 1602.
15. 7 P.S. § 311. The stock of a bank located in another state is not a permissible investment for a Pennsylvania state bank.
16. As presently defined, counties of the first class, second class and second class A include only Allegheny, Delaware, Montgomery and Philadelphia Counties.
17. Because the McFadden Act permits national banks to branch only to the same extent as state banks, national banks are similarly restricted. 12 U.S.C § 36.
18. The legislation states that "bank holding company" shall have the same meaning as it has under the BHCA.
19. Control is defined to have the same meaning as in the BHCA. Under that statute control of a bank means ownership of 25% or more of any class of voting securities of the institution.
20. Under the BHCA, there is a presumption that any company owning less than 5% of any class of voting securities of a bank does not have control of the bank. In the case of entitites which own, directly or indirectly, more than 5% but less than 25% of the voting securities of a bank, Regulation Y of the Federal Reserve Board sets forth certain indicia that give rise to a rebuttable presumption of control. The regulation also establishes an administrative procedure for determining if control exists. 12 C.F.R. § 225.31.
21. *See* note 11, *supra*.
22. A holding company is deemed to be located in the state in which the total deposits of all its bank subsidiaries are the largest. 7 P.S. § 116(a)(i).
23. For convenience of reference the term "state" shall include the District of Columbia throughout this article.

The requirement that the acquiror be located within the specified eight state region and the requirement that 75% of the deposits of the acquiror be located within this region are both eliminated after March 4, 1990.

1. *The Five Requirements.*

a. The Regional Compact for Commercial Banks and Bank Holding Companies.

Two of the five requirements in the Pennsylvania legislation are intertwined, temporary and have the effect of enlisting Pennsylvania in a regional compact.[24] The two requirements are that any out-of-state acquiror of a Pennsylvania bank holding company be located in one of the eight states (including the District of Columbia) enumerated in the legislation and the requirement that 75% of the deposits of any acquiror be located in the nine state region (the eight enumerated states plus Pennsylvania). By enacting this legislation, the Pennsylvania legislature has permitted Pennsylvania to enter an established regional compact in which Pennsylvania had been the missing link.[25] Although the various state statutes contain many different provisions, five of the eight states in the region defined by the Pennsylvania legislation previously have adopted legislation that permits, or in the near future will permit, Pennsylvania bank holding companies to enter their states on a reciprocal basis.[26] Two other states have passed interstate legislation, but at the present time, Pennsylvania is not included in the regions these statutes create.[27]

This legislation is designed to preclude the entry by acquisition or merger into Pennsylvania of bank holding companies located outside the designated region and by bank holding companies that do not have 75% of their deposits located within the region. These provisions are modeled on the provisions of other existing regional compact statutes. Their effect is to protect Pennsylvania banks and bank holding companies from acquisition (whether negotiated or nonnegotiated) by the large money center banks located in California, Illinois, and New York. Perhaps the most significant threat of takeover comes from the large institutions located in New York City. Pennsylvania is a very attractive banking market and if New York institutions are permitted to enter Pennsylvania, certain Pennsylvania bank holding companies may be vulnerable to takeover if market conditions are favorable.[28] Built into the statute is a national "trigger" which eliminates these restrictions on March 4, 1990. Thus, the legislation establishes a window during which bank holding companies

---

24. "Regional compact" is a misnomer. States do not pass a uniform law. Instead, each state enacts its own legislation which generally specifies a region in which reciprocal interstate banking is permitted. The regional compact, then, is defined by examining the various statutes and determining the extent to which defined regions overlap.

25. The validity of regional compacts was established by the United States Supreme Court in *Northeast Bancorp, Inc. v. Federal Reserve Board,* _____ U.S. _____, 105 S. Ct. 2545, 86 L. Ed. 2d 112 (1985).

26. Delaware, Kentucky, Maryland, New Jersey, Ohio and West Virginia have adopted interstate legislation that permits, or soon will permit entry by Pennsylvania bank holding companies. *See infra* Section V for a description of each state's legislation.

27. Virginia and the District of Columbia do not include Pennsylvania in their regional legislation. *See infra* Section V.

28. Lobbyists for Citicorp, in fact, persuaded a Representative to offer an amendment to the legislation which would have permitted any bank holding company to enter Pennsylvania if it makes $1 billion in loans in the Commonwealth and employs 200 people within three years after entry. The amendment was defeated.

within the region can grow and attain sufficient size and market strength to remain competitive with the large money center banks after 1990. An ancillary effect of this restriction is to prevent bank holding companies from collecting deposits through Pennsylvania branches and deploying these funds outside the region.

If an out-of-state bank holding company acquires a Pennsylvania bank or bank holding company and subsequently fails to be located within the region (by reason of another out-of-state acquisition with a resultant change in deposit concentration) or is itself acquired by an entity located outside the region, the statute requires divestiture of the holding company's Pennsylvania subsidiary. If the change in circumstances occurs voluntarily, divestiture must occur prior to the event which causes the holding company to be located outside the region. If the change in circumstances occurs other than voluntarily, divestiture must occur within one year, which period may be extended to a maximum of two years with the consent of the DOB.

The requirement that 75% of the deposits of any acquiror be located within the specified region, contains potential pitfalls which bank executives should keep in mind in planning its acquisition and antitakeover strategy. For example, an Ohio bank holding company which desires to enter the Pennsylvania market prior to 1990 (which is permissible under both Pennsylvania and Ohio law), but also desires to enter Michigan (which is permissible under both Ohio and Michigan law) must choose carefully. Because Michigan is not included within the region established under Pennsylvania law, an Ohio bank holding company must be certain that the acquisition of a Michigan institution does not cause more than 25% of its deposits to be located outside the nine state region defined by the Pennsylvania legislation. This test must be met by an acquiror immediately *before* and *after* any acquisition of a Pennsylvania institution and therefore the fact that the acquisition of a Pennsylvania institution might shift 75% or more of the deposits back within the region is not helpful. The same deposit requirement, however, can also be used as a defensive tactic. A Pennsylvania institution that does not want to be acquired by an Ohio institution can make acquisitions in a state outside the region (if such state permits the acquisition), thereby possibly insulating itself from any threat of takeover by an Ohio bank holding company.

b. Reciprocity for Bank Holding Companies.

The third requirement of Pennsylvania's interstate banking legislation is that the laws of the state in which any acquiror is located must be "reciprocal" with Pennsylvania's statute. In concept, this simply means that Pennsylvania will not allow bank holding companies located in another state to acquire Pennsylvania banks or bank holding companies unless the laws of that state permit Pennsylvania bank holding companies to acquire banks or bank holding companies located in that state. Specifically, Pennsylvania's legislation provides that the law of another state is reciprocal to the extent it expressly authorizes a Pennsylvania bank holding company to acquire a bank or bank holding company located in that state on terms and conditions substantially no more restrictive than those applicable to such an acquisition by a bank holding company located in that state. The law of a state will not fail to satisfy the reciprocity requirement if, under the laws of the state, a Pennsylvania bank holding company would be subject to limitations and restrictions on an acquisition of a bank or bank holding company that would also be applicable to a bank holding company located in that state. For example, Kentucky, New Jersey, Ohio and West Virginia all establish limitations on acquisitions that would increase deposit concentration above certain levels.[29] However, because these restrictions are also applicable to banks and bank holding companies located in those states, the legislation of these states is reciprocal within the meaning of the Pennsylvania statute and a Pennsylvania bank holding company can acquire Kentucky, New Jersey, Ohio or West Virginia banks or bank holding companies subject to these limitations. Similarly, the reciprocity requirement will not fail to be satisfied solely because of the existence of limitations and restrictions on the acquisition of a bank or bank holding company which do not materially limit the ability of a Pennsylvania bank holding company to acquire such bank or bank holding company. The law of a state will fail to satisfy the reciprocity requirement if a bank in that state which a Pennsylvania bank holding company acquires becomes subject to restrictions on competition for deposits or loans not generally applicable to other banks in the state.

The Department of Banking is authorized by the statute to determine if the law of another state satisfies the reciprocity requirement, but the statute also specifies that, as of March 31, 1986, the laws of the states of Kentucky, Maryland, Michigan, New Jersey, New York, Ohio, Rhode Island, Utah, Washington and West Virginia do satisfy the reciprocity requirement. If any of these laws subsequently are amended, the DOB is authorized to determine if reciprocity continues to exist. A number of the states whose laws are expressly deemed reciprocal under Pennsylvania law are not included in the regional compact established under the Pennsylvania law and most of these states also require reciprocity. Accordingly, until 1990, no bank holding company located in any of these states can enter Pennsylvania nor could Pennsylvania bank holding company enter those states.

    c. Department of Banking Approval.

    (1) The Application and Department of Banking Jurisdiction.

The approval process for an interstate acquisition requires submission of an application to the DOB and a review by the DOB of the credit practices and transaction account services provided by the acquiror in Pennsylvania.

Under the new Pennsylvania interstate commercial banking legislation, the Pennsylvania Department of Banking must approve any interstate acquisition. Both an acquiror located outside of Pennsylvania which desires to acquire a Pennsylvania institution and a Pennsylvania bank holding company which desires to make an out of state acquisition must submit an application to the DOB.[30] In both cases, the

---

29. Kentucky prohibits acquisitions that would result in an institution holding 15% or more of all the deposits in Kentucky banks. In Ohio and West Virginia, acquisitions resulting in an institution with deposits equal to or greater than 20% of deposits for all financial institutions (banks and thrifts) in the state are prohibited. In New Jersey, acquisitions which cause deposit concentrations for one institution to exceed 12% of deposits of all New Jersey financial institutions (banks and thrifts) are prohibited. (This percentage is scheduled to increase to 13.5%).

30. The form of application for the acquisition of a Pennsylvania bank or bank holding company by an

DOB must approve or disapprove the proposed acquisition by written notice to the applicant within the later of sixty days after receipt of the application or thirty days after receipt of any additional information requested by the DOB. Any approval can be made subject to such terms and conditions as the DOB may deem appropriate in order to carry out the provisions of the legislation. This approval process is unlikely to significantly affect the timetable for the consummation of most merger or acquisition transactions.

The jurisdiction which the Pennsylvania legislature has granted the DOB is exceptionally broad. The legislation requires the DOB to approve the acquisition of any institution or Pennsylvania bank holding company by a bank holding company located outside of Pennsylvania. The legislation defines an institution to be any state bank, state bank and trust company or national bank whose principal place of business is located in Pennsylvania.[31] Accordingly, the DOB has jurisdiction over an acquisition of a national bank located in Pennsylvania by a bank holding company located in and chartered under the laws of any other state. Although the DOB's power to review such a transaction is quite broad, under existing law it presently has the same review power over an intrastate acquisition by a bank holding company of a national bank.[32]

A similar result arises in connection with the acquisition of a bank or bank holding company located outside of Pennsylvania by a Pennsylvania bank holding company. A Pennsylvania bank holding company is defined as a bank holding company whose banking subsidiaries' operations are principally conducted in Pennsylvania as determined by the state in which its deposit concentration is the largest.[33] This definition includes bank holding companies whose only subsidiaries are national banks. Furthermore, because it is the location of the banking subsidiaries that makes a bank holding company a "Pennsylvania bank holding company," the holding company need not even be incorporated in Pennsylvania. Thus, a bank holding company incorporated in Delaware with a national banking subsidiary located in Pennsylvania would need DOB approval for the acquisition of a national bank in New Jersey. In short, Pennsylvania exerts jurisdiction over any interstate transaction involving a party *located* in Pennsylvania, regardless of the type of charter or the place of incorporation of the Pennsylvania party.

(2) The Scope of Review.

Although Pennsylvania retains jurisdiction over entry into Pennsylvania by out-of-state bank holding companies and out-of-state acquisitions by Pennsylvania bank holding companies, the standard of review utilized in the approval process is different. The standard of review for interstate acquisitions by Pennsylvania bank holding companies is limited to a determination of the effect of the acquisition on the continued availability in Pennsylvania of certain basic banking services while the

---

out-of-state bank holding company is set forth in Exhibit "G-1." The form of application for the acquisition of an out-of-state bank or bank holding company by a Pennsylvania bank holding company is set forth in Exhibit "G-2." The instructions for both forms are set forth in Exhibit "G-3."
31. 7 P.S. §§ 115(a)(ii) and 116(a)(iii).
32. 7 P.S. § 112(b).
33. 7 P.S. § 115(a)(iii).

scope of review for entry into Pennsylvania by out-of-state institutions includes certain additional criteria discussed in detail below.

The common criteria for both entry into Pennsylvania by bank holding companies located outside Pennsylvania and interstate acquisitions by Pennsylvania bank holding companies is the availability in Pennsylvania of credit for individuals and business and the extent to which basic checking or transaction accounts are made available to the public. With respect to out-of-state acquisitions by Pennsylvania bank holding companies, the focus of this review is on the Pennsylvania bank holding company's banking subsidiaries located in Pennsylvania. The DOB is to evaluate the effect the acquisition will have on the basic services offered by the Pennsylvania subsidiaries in the future and assure that the reasonable availability of such services will not be diminished. Both the statute and the application promulgated by the DOB are silent as to what "reasonable availability" means. Presumably the DOB possesses the ability to alter the standard from time to time. Although the DOB will have broad power to review credit practices and transaction account services, most institutions do provide basic credit and transaction account services and therefore it is unlikely that this will significantly impede interstate transactions.

With respect to an acquisition of a Pennsylvania institution by a bank holding company located outside Pennsylvania, the focus of review is on the effect the acquisition will have on the the availability of banking services offered by the Pennsylvania acquiree. Again, the DOB is empowered to assure the continued availability of these basic services but the statute and application are silent as to the level of availability which must be maintained. These provisions concerning basic banking services will have the most immediate effect on Pennsylvania bank holding companies rather than out-of-state acquirors. This is because these provisions will affect *all* Pennsylvania banking subsidiaries of a Pennsylvania bank holding company which makes an interstate acquisition but a bank holding company located outside Pennsylvania will only have to comply with these provisions with respect to its new Pennsylvania subsidiary. However, over time, as more and more banking institutions located in Pennsylvania become part of an interstate organization, these provisions will touch the majority of Pennsylvania banks.

The provisions concerning credit availability and basic transaction account services are applicable to both out-of-state acquirors of Pennsylvania banks and bank holding companies and Pennsylvania bank holding companies seeking to acquire an out-of-state entity. Bank holding companies seeking to enter Pennsylvania, however, are also subject to additional review before the DOB will approve the acquisition. The interstate legislation requires the DOB to evaluate the application on the basis of (i) the financial and managerial resources of the applicant, (ii) the financial history and future prospects of the applicant and each Pennsylvania bank or bank holding company to be acquired, (iii) any undue concentration of resources which would result from the acquisition, and (iv) the convenience and needs of the public.[34] Completely unexplained by the legislation is what is meant by "undue concentration of resources." Presumably, the legislature was seeking to address

---

34. The convenience and needs of the public encompasses, without limitation, the credit and basic transaction account availability review.

antitrust concerns but no test is specified nor is there any clue as to whether the defined relevant geographic market will change as a result of the regional compact.[35] Presumably similar antitrust tests will be applied, albeit on a less parochial level. In general, however, this list of criteria is a familiar one to bankers because it is similar to the criteria presently utilized by the DOB and federal regulators in assessing bank mergers and acquisitions by bank holding companies. Accordingly, except for any requirements imposed in connection with the credit and basic transaction account availability rules, the criteria should not erect any new regulatory hurdles or require any additional compliance.

(3) Review of credit practices.

The credit practices which the DOB is required to examine in connection with any interstate acquisition differ for individuals and businesses. For individuals, the DOB's examination is to include, but not be limited to, the availability of consumer loans, residential mortgages, home improvement loans and student loans with particular emphasis on the availability of such loans to residents of low and moderate income neighborhoods. For businesses, the DOB's review is to include, but not be limited to, the availability of credit and investments intended to promote economic development and the creation or retention of jobs. Particular emphasis is to be placed on the availability of Small Business Administration and other small business loans, industrial development loans, loans to employee stock ownership plans, loans to finance leveraged buyouts by employees, loans to nonprofit community development projects, and loans to promote the international trade and exports of Pennsylvania businesses. It is important to note that the legislation does not specify any standard of availability for these credit services. There is no requirement that an institution make a certain dollar value of any particular type of loan. Of course, it is unlikely that the DOB would be satisfied if an institution merely offers these products without actually making any loans.

The DOB review of an institution's credit practices is to be made in light of its financial condition, the existing competition, the needs of its community[36] and the availability of alternative sources of credit. If, as a result of its review, the DOB determines that the Pennsylvania institution involved in the interstate transaction has not been materially deficient in its performance with regard to the availability of credit and such performance justifies the conclusion that the Pennsylvania institution will provide suitable credit to its community in the future, then the application can be approved. If the Pennsylvania institution is found to be deficient or the DOB cannot conclude that the institution will provide suitable credit to its community in the future, the DOB may approve the transaction subject to such terms and conditions as it deems appropriate to improve the performance of the institution over a stated period of time. It is interesting to note that the DOB is not given express authority to disapprove an application for failure to meet the credit needs of its

---

35. At present, Standard Metropolitan Statistical Areas are generally the defined geographic market for bank holding companies subject to regulation by the Federal Reserve Board. However, with the advent of interstate banking and the resulting interstate consolidation an argument can be made that this geographic market definition is too restrictive.
36. "Community" is not defined by the legislation although it clearly includes only communities located in Pennsylvania.

community. It might be presumed that this power is implied, but if the DOB ever completely denies an application, litigation would likely follow. As a practical matter, if the DOB did object to the credit practices of an applicant, negotiations between the applicant and the DOB would likely result.

The legislation also instructs the DOB to review from time to time the performance of each institution involved in an interstate acquisition to ensure continued satisfactory credit performance and to issue corrective orders where necessary. The legislation contains no time limit on the right of the DOB to review credit performance. However, no specific enforcement powers are granted by the legislation in order to ensure compliance. Rather, the DOB is empowered simply to issue regulations and orders to enforce these provisions. No specific sanctions for a violation of any order is specified. Accordingly, although the legislation purports to give the DOB the power to review forever the credit practices of any Pennsylvania institution which was ever involved in an interstate acquisition, because the DOB is not granted any right to enforce its orders through coercive sanctions, the DOB's real power may lie in its ability to approve or disapprove future transactions involving the applicant.

(4) Review of basic transaction account services.

The legislation grants the DOB the authority to ensure that bank holding companies and institutions which become part of an interstate banking organization make basic account services available to the public. To that end, the DOB is instructed to collect information with respect to the needs of the public, especially low and moderate income individuals, for basic checking or other transaction accounts, the nature and amount of charges for such accounts and the existing availability of such accounts in the various communities throughout the state. This collected information presumably will be used as a reference point in reviewing any application for approval of an acquisition and in establishing standards that must be met by Pennsylvania institutions in the future.

An applicant seeking approval of an interstate acquisition must provide the DOB with information concerning the basic transaction accounts offered by the applicant's existing or proposed Pennsylvania banking subsidiaries. This information must include (i) the number of checks and deposit transactions allowed per month and the charges pertaining thereto, (ii) the "hold" periods placed upon accounts for deposited checks, (iii) the types and amounts of other charges imposed, (iv) the form of identification required to use and open such accounts, and (v) the method by which the availability of such accounts is made known to the public. The DOB may approve the application prior to receipt of any requested information but each Pennsylvania institution that is a subsidiary of the applicant shall be subject, both before and after the acquisition, to such requirements as the DOB may impose from time to time to ensure that the community served by the Pennsylvania institution has the basic transaction account services that the DOB determines is necessary. An out-of-state applicant seeking to acquire a Pennsylvania institution will only have to supply information to the DOB with respect to its Pennsylvania acquiree. However, the DOB could examine the transaction account policies of the applicant's out-of-state subsidiary in connection with its general power to examine the affairs of the acquiror.

Again, this provision of the legislation purports to give the DOB far-reaching powers. The DOB is empowered to require that any subsidiary of a Pennsylvania bank holding company which makes an interstate acquisition or any Pennsylvania bank which is acquired by a holding company located outside Pennsylvania provide certain basic account services to its community. This could include the establishment by the DOB of the exact nature and level of transaction account services (such as checking or NOW accounts) which an institution must provide and the fees chargeable in connection therewith. Again, there is no time limit on the ability of the DOB to impose prospective requirements. Moreover, the legislation clearly contemplates that the standards established by the DOB can be changed at any time if the DOB determines that the needs of the public have changed. However, as noted above, the DOB has no specific coercive sanctions which it can impose in order to enforce any orders it may issue in connection with this review power.

Only the state of Maryland has passed interstate legislation containing provisions similar to the Pennsylvania provisions concerning the availability of credit and basic transaction account services. Because all other statutes enacted by states in the region defined by the Pennsylvania legislation require reciprocity, the possibility exists that some of these jurisdictions could declare Pennsylvania's legislation nonreciprocal because of these consumer provisions. However, these provisions should not materially affect the operations of most acquirors and therefore the likelihood that the Pennsylvania statute would be declared nonreciprocal seems remote. Furthermore, the possibility that Pennsylvania's statute would be deemed nonreciprocal by another state is mitigated somewhat by the fact that Pennsylvania bank holding companies that make interstate acquisitions are subject to the same provisions. However, this fact does not fully satisfy most state reciprocity requirements because Pennsylvania bank holding companies that acquire other *Pennsylvania* institutions are *not* expressly made subject to these provisions. Finally, in lieu of declaring Pennsylvania's statute nonreciprocal, other states could impose similar restrictions on Pennsylvania bank holding companies which make acquisitions in their state.

d. *Subsidiary Limitation.*

Prior to 1986, Pennsylvania bank holding companies could only own four banking subsidiaries located in Pennsylvania. Currently Pennsylvania bank holding companies can own eight banking subsidiaries located in Pennsylvania. In 1990 this limitation will be eliminated entirely.[37] Under the interstate legislation out-of-state acquirors will be subject to the same limitations. No distinction is made based on the location of the subsidiaries. As a practical matter, this restriction has not seriously impeded the expansion efforts of Pennsylvania bank holding companies because of the time required to assimilate acquisitions and because a holding company can always cause its subsidiaries to merge in order to stay within the limit. Moreover, most bank holding companies have been able to enter the principal Pennsylvania markets while staying within the limit. Now that the limit on banking subsidiaries located in Pennsylvania which can be owned by a bank holding company has been increased to eight, the restrictive effect on Pennsylvania institutions

---

37. 7 P.S. § 115.

can be expected to diminish further. Certain out-of-state regional holding companies which engage in aggressive acquisition campaigns could be somewhat hampered. These institutions can mitigate the effect of this restriction by merging subsidiaries or by entering into stakeout agreements[38] pursuant to which an acquiror and acquiree agree to consummate an acquisition at a future date when it is legally permitted. Finally, it should be noted that this subsidiary limitation should not adversely affect any reciprocity determination made by other jurisdictions concerning Pennsylvania's statute since it is equally applicable to holding companies located within and without Pennsylvania.

D. Interstate Expansion Under the New Legislation.

If statutorily permitted, interstate expansion theoretically could occur through the *de novo* branching of state or national banks, mergers between state or national banks, acquisitions by state or national banks, mergers between bank holding companies, or acquisitions by bank holding companies of other bank holding companies or state or national banks. The new legislation authorizes only mergers between bank holding companies or acquisitions by bank holding companies of other bank holding companies or state or national banks. State-chartered banks located in Pennsylvania cannot branch, merge or make acquisitions[39] across state lines nor can banks located outside Pennsylvania enter the Commonwealth by any of these methods. Federal legislation similarly constrains national banks. Thus, the new legislation only authorizes interstate expansion in a limited manner. Nevertheless, because of the provisions of the Douglas Amendment to the BHCA and the fact that most expansion-oriented banking organizations are structured as holding companies, the legislation will have far-reaching effects. The following is a chart of the methods of interstate expansion both into and out of Pennsylvania permitted for banking organizations under federal law and the new Pennsylvania law:

(see next page)

---

38. A stakeout agreement, in addition to being a contract to effect an acquisition when legally permitted, also often involves the purchase of convertible securities of the acquiree by the acquiror in order to "lock-up" the target and restrict its ability to negotiate a transaction with another entity. Shareholder approval of the proposed transaction can be solicited either before or after the acquisition becomes legally permissible.

39. Because a bank that acquires and operates another bank as a subsidiary becomes a bank holding company, it might be argued that a bank could make an interstate acquisition. However, because the bank would not be a holding company when it filed its application, approval would be unlikely.

	Permissible Activity		
	Branching	**Merger**	**Acquisition**
National Bank located in Pennsylvania	No[40]	No[41]	No[42]
Pennsylvania State Bank	No[43]	No[44]	No[45]
Operating Bank Subsidiary of Bank Holding Company[46] (i.e. not an interim bank)	No	No	No
Bank Holding Company	N/A	Yes[47]	Yes[48]

---

40. National banks are prohibited from branching across state lines by the McFadden Act, 12 U.S.C. § 36. National banks are permitted, however, to relocate their main office to within 30 miles of their original main office. In the important case of *McEnteer v. Clark*, ___F. Supp. ___(E.D. Pa. 1986), a federal court upheld the relocation of Horizon Bancorp's only office from Moorestown, New Jersey, to Philadelphia despite the objections of the DOB. If this decision is upheld on appeal, national banks could use this decision creatively to expand interstate. It might also cause state banks to change their charters to national charters.

41. Interstate mergers of national banks is prohibited by federal law, 12 U.S.C. 215, 215a and 215b.

42. Pursuant to 12 U.S.C. § 24, Seventh, a national bank is not permitted to invest in stock of another corporation except to the extent enumerated therein. Stock of another bank is not a permissible investment except under certain limited circumstances. Ostensibly then, a national bank cannot acquire another bank. Section 24, Seventh, however, grants a national bank the power to exercise all powers incidental to banking. Both the Comptroller of the Currency (with respect to national banks) and the Federal Reserve Board (with respect to state member banks) have permitted banks to own the stock of subsidiaries that carry on functions which the bank itself could do. Based on these interpretations, a national bank or state member bank theoretically could acquire another bank since as a bank, it could certainly carry on the activity of the acquiree institution. Despite this apparent ability of a national bank to acquire another bank, Pennsylvania legislation does not permit a national bank located outside of Pennsylvania to acquire a Pennsylvania institution. Because most states require reciprocity, a national bank located in Pennsylvania could not acquire an out-of-state bank.

43. Pennsylvania state banks are prohibited from branching across state lines under Section 904 of the Banking Code of 1965, 7 P.S. § 904. Under Sections 904 and 905 of the Banking Code of 1965, 7 P.S. §§ 904 and 905, an out-of-state, state chartered bank could not receive permission to establish a branch in Pennsylvania.

44. Pennsylvania state banks cannot merge across state lines under Section 1602 of the Pennsylvania Banking Code of 1965, 7 P.S. § 1602. As a result, an out-of-state, state chartered bank cannot merge with a Pennsylvania state bank.

45. The stock of a bank located outside Pennsylvania is not a permitted investment for a Pennsylvania bank under Section 311 of the Banking Code of 1965 and therefore an interstate acquisition by a Pennsylvania state bank would not be permitted, 7 P.S. § 311. An out-of-state, state chartered bank would be denied permission to acquire a Pennsylvania institution under Section 112 of the Banking Code of 1965, 7 P.S. § 112.

46. The rules for an operating bank subsidiary of a holding company are the same as the rules for a bank having the same type of charter (national or state) which is not a subsidiary of a holding company. It appears, however, that the rule for an interim bank chartered solely for purposes of effecting an acquisition are different. See note 49.

47. Senate Bill 1075 authorizes interstate mergers of bank holding companies. Although the statute uses the term "acquire," it is defined to include any transaction that would be deemed an acquisition under the BHCA and the regulations promulgated thereunder. A merger of bank holding companies would qualify as an acquisition under the BHCA. A bank holding company cannot merge with a national or state bank.

48. Senate Bill 1075 and the Douglas Amendment to the BHCA permit bank holding companies located outside Pennsylvania to make acquisitions in Pennsylvania if the laws of the home state of the acquiror are reciprocal. Accordingly, Pennsylvania bank holding companies also can make interstate acquisitions in states which have passed reciprocal legislation. The method of acquisition of a holding company could be a tender or exchange offer or other purchase of the stock or assets of a bank or bank holding company. With respect to a bank, a holding company could charter an interim bank in the target's home state and effect a merger of the interim bank and the target. Although this could be deemed to be an impermissible

III. THE THRIFT LEGISLATION

A. The Existing Federal Legislative Scheme.

Until recently, no federal savings and loan, federal savings bank or savings and loan holding company could expand interstate except in connection with the acquisition of a failed or failing savings bank[49] because FHLBB regulations prohibited such activity for federal thrifts and the Savings and Loan Holding Company Act ("SLHCA") contains a prohibition against formation of a holding company controlling insured institutions in more than one state.[50] The FHLBB has recently adopted a new interstate branching regulation which permits federal thrifts to expand interstate. This regulation is discussed in detail in Part IV. The SLHCA prohibition against multi-state savings and loan holding companies still remains, however, and the existence of this prohibition greatly affects the method of interstate expansion of thrifts.

B. Pennsylvania's Pre-existing Legislation.

The activities of Pennsylvania-chartered savings banks are regulated by the Banking Code of 1965. Accordingly, prior to passage of the interstate thrift bills, Pennsylvania savings banks could not branch except into bicontiguous counties or into Allegheny, Delaware, Montgomery or Philadelphia Counties;[51] savings banks could not enter into interstate mergers;[52] nor could savings banks make interstate acquisitions.[53] Pennsylvania state savings and loan associations are governed by the Savings Association Code of 1967.[54] Although regulated by a different statute, prior to passage of the interstate thrift bills, savings and loan associations also possessed no interstate rights. Pennsylvania state savings and loan associations could branch on a statewide basis but could not branch,[55] merge[56] or make

---

interstate establishment of a *de novo* bank, Pennsylvania will permit this method of acquiring a Pennsylvania bank and presumably other states will as well.

49. Under a provision of the Garn-St. Germain Depository Institutions Act of 1982 amending the SLHCA, interstate acquisitions were permitted, 12 U.S.C. § 1730(m). This provision expired on October 13, 1986 but, at this writing both the House and the Senate have enacted H.R. 431 extending this legislation until September 15, 1987. However, because the Senate amended H.R. 431 (with respect to a matter unrelated to supervisory acquisitions), final passage of the legislation awaits resolution of differences by a House-Senate conference committee. Under this expired statute, banks and bank holding companies could also acquire failed or failing thrifts across state lines although preference was given by the FHLBB to acquisitions by thrifts (whether in or out of state) or banks or bank holding companies located in the state of the failed or failing institutions.

50. 12 U.S.C. § 1730a(e)(3). The complete text of the SLHCA, including the expired amendment added by the Garn-St. Germain Depository Institutions Act of 1982, is set forth in Exhibit "H."

51. 7 P.S. § 904.

52. 7 P.S. § 1609.

53. 7 P.S. § 311.

54. 7 P.S. § 6020-1 *et seq.*

55. Before enactment of the interstate thrift legislation, Section 403 of the Savings Association Code permitted statewide branching but did not permit interstate branching, 7 P.S. § 6020-53.

56. Section 1101 of the Savings Association Code permits mergers between Pennsylvania state savings associations and Pennsylvania savings banks and between a Pennsylvania savings association and a Pennsylvania savings bank. In addition, Section 1101 permits mergers between either a Pennsylvania savings and loan or savings bank and *any* federal savings association or federal savings bank. Thus, under

acquisitions[57] across state lines. Finally, holding companies which own state savings banks are subject to the eight subsidiary limitation contained in the Banking Code of 1965 but thrift holding companies which own savings associations are not subject to any such restriction because no similar provision exists in the Savings Association Code of 1967.[58] The new legislation sweeps away almost all these rules and allows interstate branching, mergers and acquisitions.

C. The New Legislation.

The savings bank legislation permits a regional thrift institution[59] or regional thrift institution holding company[60] to acquire[61] a Pennsylvania savings bank[62] or a Pennsylvania savings bank holding company[63] if three conditions are met. The savings association legislation requires that the same three conditions be met before a regional thrift institution or a regional thrift institution holding company[64] can acquire[65] a Pennsylvania association[66] or a Pennsylvania association holding com-

---

Pennsylvania law a Pennsylvania association or savings bank could merge with a federal thrift located outside Pennsylvania if it were permissible under federal law. However, even under the FHLBB's new interstate regulation, prior to passage of the thrift bills no interstate merger between a federal association or savings bank and a state association or savings bank would have been permissible because the regulation only permits such a transaction if it were permissible between two state institutions.

57. The stock of an out-of-state association is not a permissible investment for a Pennsylvania association under Sections 701 and 922 of the Savings Association Code, 7 P.S. §§ 6020-102 and 6020-162. Section 701 does permit a state association to invest in any capital stock in which a federal association could invest in but since such a transaction could not be entered into by a federal association even under the new regulation, a state association cannot make interstate acquisitions.

58. Unlike national banks and bank holding companies, until recently the interstate rights of federal thrifts and thrift holding companies did not depend on the interstate rights of state institutions. The new FHLBB regulation concerning interstate branching does tie the rights of federal thrifts (but not thrift holding companies) to their state brethren.

59. A "regional thrift institution" is defined to include a state or federally-chartered savings bank located in the region and a state or federally-chartered savings and loan association located in the region, whether stock or mutual. Under the statute, a thrift institution is deemed to be located in the state in which its deposit concentration is the largest.

60. A "regional thrift institution holding company" is defined as an entity that controls one or more regional thrift institutions and is located in the region. A thrift holding company is deemed to be located in the state in which the deposit concentration of its subsidiaries is the largest and "control" means the power, directly or indirectly, to direct the management or policies of an entity or to vote 25% or more of any class of voting securities of an entity.

61. "Acquire" is defined to mean the acquisition of 5% or more of the voting stock of an entity and also means a merger or consolidation or a purchase of assets and an assumption of liabilities other than in the regular course of business and would include a merger conversion, stock for stock swap, or the purchase of a branch.

62. A "Pennsylvania savings bank" is defined to have the meaning set forth in Section 102 of the Pennsylvania Banking Code of 1965, 7 P.S. §102(x).

63. A "Pennsylvania savings bank holding company" is defined to be an entity that controls one or more Pennsylvania savings banks and is located in Pennsylvania.

64. A "regional thrift institution" and a "regional thrift institution holding company" have the same meaning in the savings association bill as they do in the savings bank bill.

65. "Acquire" has the same meaning in the savings association bill as in the savings bank bill.

66. A "Pennsylvania association" is defined to include an association, as defined in Section 102(3) of the Pennsylvania Savings Association Code of 1967, 7 P.S. §6020-2, and a federal association, as defined in 12 U.S.C. §1462(d), that is located in Pennsylvania.

pany.[67] These three conditions are:

>(i) the laws of the acquiror's home state (and the laws of the state of any entity which controls the acquiror) must allow Pennsylvania thrift institutions or Pennsylvania thrift institution holding companies to enter that state;

>(ii) the acquiror or any entity which controls the acquiror, must be located in Delaware, Kentucky, Maryland, New Jersey, Ohio, Pennsylvania, Virginia, West Virginia or the District of Columbia; and

>(iii) the Pennsylvania Department of Banking must approve the acquisition.[68]

Both the new savings bank and savings association legislation also permit *de novo* branching across state lines by regional savings banks and savings associations. Finally, both the savings bank and the savings association legislation permit Pennsylvania savings banks and savings associations to branch anywhere in Pennsylvania or the United States with approval of the Department of Banking. Of course, the ability of Pennsylvania thrifts to branch into another state will depend on the laws of that jurisdiction. Because most state statutes require some degree of reciprocity, and Pennsylvania only extends branching rights to those states in the designated region, this nationwide branching ability currently may be more illusory than real. For example, under the legislation, a Pennsylvania thrift could establish a branch in New York but because New York institutions cannot establish a branch in Pennsylvania, New York's legislation would not permit the establishment of a branch in New York by a Pennsylvania thrift.[69]

The extent of the legislative change for Pennsylvania thrifts is dramatic and because the rights of federal thrifts are now linked to the rights of their state brethren, they are equally affected. Under Pennsylvania law, thrift institutions will be able to expand within the region by any means they choose. Only the SLHCA's prohibition against multi-state savings and loan holding companies will impose any significant barrier to interstate expansion.

1. The Three Requirements.

a. The Regional Compact for Thrifts.

The two thrift bills create the same region as the commercial banking legislation. Although Pennsylvania was one of the last states within this region to enact interstate banking legislation, was one of the leaders in such legislation for thrifts.

---

67. A "Pennsylvania association holding company" is defined as an entity that controls one or more Pennsylvania associations and is located in Pennsylvania. The definitions of "control" and "located" are identical to the definitions contained in the savings bank legislation.

68. Under the Garn-St. Germain Depository Institutions Act of 1982, the FSLIC may permit the interstate acquisition of failing FSLIC-insured, state-chartered thrifts and under certain circumstances the objections of the appropriate state official can be overridden, 12 U.S.C. §1730a(m). As stated in Note 50, this provision has expired but is expected to be re-enacted.

69. See Section V for a discussion of the reciprocity requirements of the states within the region established by Pennsylvania's legislation which have enacted interstate thrift legislation.

Maryland, New Jersey, Ohio, Virginia and West Virginia also have passed interstate legislation for thrifts. Delaware has enacted interstate legislation for saving banks but not savings associations. Kentucky and the District of Columbia have no interstate thrift legislation although all District of Columbia thrifts are federally-chartered and therefore have certain rights under the FHLBB's interstate regulation.[70]

Noticeably absent from the thrift legislation is the "trigger" provision contained in the commercial banking legislation which would eliminate after a stated period the requirement that any entity seeking to enter Pennsylvania be located in the region defined by the legislation. This absence of a trigger provision may insulate Pennsylvania thrifts from a significant amount of competition.[71] It may also hinder the expansion of Pennsylvania thrifts into states outside the region whose statutes require reciprocity, but presumably the Pennsylvania General Assembly will be willing to change the legislation when this occurs.

In the event that an out-of-state thrift acquires a Pennsylvania thrift and subsequently fails to be located within the region (because of a change in deposit concentration) or is itself acquired by an entity located outside the region, the statute requires divestiture of the thrift's Pennsylvania branches or subsidiaries. If the change in circumstances occurs voluntarily, divestiture must occur prior to the event which causes the thrift to be located outside the region. If the change in circumstances occurs other than voluntarily, divestiture must occur within one year, which period may be extended to a maximum of two years with the consent of the DOB.

b. Reciprocity for Thrifts.

With respect to acquisitions, the test for determining if another state's legislation is reciprocal has two elements: (i) the law of the other state must authorize Pennsylvania thrift institutions to make acquisitions in that state on terms and conditions reasonably equivalent to those applicable to acquisitions of Pennsylvania thrift institutions by regional thrift institutions, and (ii) the law of the other state must not impose conditions on acquisitions by Pennsylvania thrift institutions that are substantially more onerous than those imposed on the same acquisitions by thrift institutions in that state. With regard to interstate branching, the test has the same two elements: the law of the other state must authorize Pennsylvania thrift institutions to establish branches on terms and conditions reasonably equivalent to those applicable to the establishment of branches in Pennsylvania by regional thrift institutions. Second, the law governing branching by Pennsylvania thrift institutions into a state must be on terms and conditions reasonably equivalent to those applicable to intrastate branching by thrift institutions located in that state.

Although the commercial banking legislation only contains the second prong of the two-part reciprocity test applicable to thrifts, the DOB has more discretion in determining if the interstate thrift legislation of another state is reciprocal. The DOB is permitted to find that the interstate thrift legislation of another state is reciprocal even if the legislation does not permit Pennsylvania thrift institutions to engage in

---

70. See Section V.
71. *But see* the discussion in Section IV concerning the FHLBB's interstate regulation and the potential for nationwide expansion through the acquisition of failed or failing institutions.

a particular type of acquisition or branching or the legislation imposes conditions on such acquisition or branching that are more onerous than conditions imposed on thrift institutions located in that state. The DOB may make this determination, however, only after it imposes similar restrictions and limitations on acquisitions and branching in Pennsylvania by thrift institutions located in that state.[72] For example, under Delaware law, only savings banks but not savings associations can enter Delaware. Accordingly, Pennsylvania could similarly prohibit entry into Pennsylvania by Delaware savings associations yet still permit entry by Delaware savings banks.

The DOB also may find a lack of reciprocity in another state's legislation if such legislation imposes different standards on acquisition and branching for different Pennsylvania institutions. For example, if the legislation of another state granted different rights to Pennsylvania thrift institutions based on their size or location, the DOB could find the law nonreciprocal. Finally, the DOB must find another state's legislation to be nonreciprocal if it discriminates between Pennsylvania-chartered institutions and federally-chartered institutions.

c. Department of Banking Approval.

The pending thrift legislation requires approval of the DOB for any interstate transaction. However, unlike the commercial banking legislation, this legislation makes no distinction between the criteria that the DOB is instructed to use in approving the acquisition of a Pennsylvania thrift institution by an out-of-state entity and an out-of-state acquisition by a Pennsylvania entity.

The only criteria which the DOB is specifically instructed to utilize is the effect the transaction will have on the availability in Pennsylvania of credit and basic transaction account services. The DOB is not instructed to consider the financial history and prospects of the acquiror or the effect the acquisition will have on deposit concentrations. Although the legislation does not contain any specific instructions to consider these factors, neither is the scope of review circumscribed in any way and the DOB could presumably claim such authority under other statutes.[73] Accordingly, absent some challenge to the statutory authority of the DOB to review these factors in a given transaction, their review is likely to encompass these matters as well.

With respect to interstate branching, the DOB is instructed to use its existing standards in determining whether to approve branching into Pennsylvania by an out-of-state thrift. The DOB would presumably use these same standards in considering a proposed interstate branch by a Pennsylvania thrift.

The guidelines for determining the availability of basic credit and transaction account services for thrifts are virtually identical to those set forth in the commercial banking legislation and discussed in detail above. The only substantive difference

---

72. The manner in which the DOB is to impose these conditions is not specified but presumably it could do so by regulation or on a case-by-case basis in connection with a specific application.
73. *See, e.g.*, Section 1609, of the Banking Code with respect to savings banks, 7 P.S. § 1609, and Section 1106 of the Savings Association Code, 7 P.S. § 6020-186.

is that in analyzing the credit practices of a given institution, the DOB is instructed to take into account the institution's status as a thrift. Although many banks and thrifts have very similar loan portfolios, others still serve essentially different markets with many banks involved principally in commercial lending and many thrifts serving primarily the home and other real estate mortgage lending markets. Accordingly, a distinction in the analysis of credit services is often appropriate.

D. The Effect of the SLHCA.

A major difference between the commercial bank legislation and the thrift legislation is that the commercial banking legislation only permits bank holding companies to expand into Pennsylvania through acquisition or merger. The thrift legislation permits thrift holding companies and thrifts to expand into Pennsylvania through branching, merger or acquisition. Thus, under the legislation, a national bank, a state-chartered bank, or a subsidiary of a bank holding company located outside Pennsylvania cannot merge with or acquire a Pennsylvania institution or establish a branch in Pennsylvania.[74] By contrast, under the thrift legislation (and without regard to certain other statutory restraints) a federally-chartered thrift, a state-chartered thrift and a federal or state-chartered subsidiary of a thrift holding company could expand into Pennsylvania either by merger, acquisition or *de novo* branching.

In large part, the reason for this distinction, lies in governing federal law. All the regional statutes permit bank holding companies (but not banks) to merge or make acquisitions across state lines. In Pennsylvania, the original draft of the legislation would have permitted banks to exercise the same powers granted to holding companies. The Department of Banking objected to this provision because it would necessitate interstate examination of banks and therefore raise jurisdictional questions. Accordingly, the legislation was changed to its present form. The identical concern could be raised with respect to thrifts, but because the SLHCA prohibits a savings and loan holding company from owning an FSLIC or FDIC-insured thrift in more than one state, a similar restriction on thrifts would actually preclude almost all interstate transactions among thrifts.

Also, the SLHCA actually prohibits certain activity ostensibly permitted under Pennsylvania's interstate thrift legislation. The Pennsylvania thrift statutes and the laws of certain other jurisdictions would appear to permit out-of-state thrift holding companies to enter their respective states through acquisition. However, the SLHCA would not permit this if it resulted in the holding company owning thrifts in more than one state. Similarly, under Pennsylvania and certain other state legislation a subsidiary of a thrift holding company could make acquisitions across state lines. Under federal law, however, the acquiror's parent, as a result of the acquisition, would become a savings and loan holding company which, albeit indirectly, controls thrifts in more than one state and consequently this transaction would be prohibited.

---

74. Of course, a holding company could be formed in connection with an interstate acquisition by a state or national bank. In addition, the use of interim banks to effect a merger appears permissible. See note 48.

Thus, as a practical matter, interstate rights that are granted by the new Pennsylvania legislation to both thrifts and thrift holding companies are in general exercisable only by thrifts.

E. Other Differences Between the Commercial Bank and Thrift Legislation.

In addition to the differences in the type of permissible interstate expansion by banks and thrifts caused by the differences between the BHCA and the SLHCA, other major differences exist. One major difference between the commercial banking legislation and the thrift legislation is the absence of a national trigger provision in the thrift bills which would eliminate the regional restrictions and open Pennsylvania to full interstate competition among thrifts. After March 4, 1990, the requirement that an acquiror of a Pennsylvania commercial bank or bank holding company be located in the region expires and commercial banks will in all likelihood be faced with competition from large banks located outside the region. Thrifts, on the other hand, may continue to enjoy the competitive protection which a regional compact provides and therefore be immune from nonnegotiated tender or exchange offers made by thrifts located outside the region, absent further regulatory changes.

In some respects, this protection may be temporary because of the FHLBB's new regulation concerning interstate branching which is designed to encourage the acquisition of failing thrifts by healthy thrifts and other regional developments.[75] This regulation permits a healthy thrift or thrift holding company which acquires a failing thrift to designate, in conjunction with the acquisition, three other states which it desires to enter. If the FHLBB approves the merger application, the acquiror can then acquire healthy thrifts in the designated states. The FHLBB has recently approved an application under this provision that affects Pennsylvania. In consideration of the acquisition of two failing Ohio thrifts, the FHLBB has granted First Nationwide Savings of San Francisco permission to expand into Colorado and Pennsylvania. First Nationwide has $12 billion dollars in assets and, if it chooses to expand into Pennsylvania, may provide formidable competition to Pennsylvania thrifts and banks as well.

Another difference between the commercial banking legislation and the thrift legislation is the rules concerning deposit concentration. Until 1990, an out-of-state bank holding company located outside Pennsylvania cannot acquire a Pennsylvania bank holding company unless 75% of the acquiror's deposits are located within the specified region. Regional thrift institutions and regional thrift holding companies, on the other hand, can make acquisitions in Pennsylvania provided they are located in the region. A thrift institution or holding company is considered to be located in the region if its or its subsidiary's deposits are largest in a state within the region. There is no requirement that this be a majority of the deposits. Thus, until 1990,

---

75. 12 C.F.R. § 556.5. See Exhibit "D." Because the FSLIC has recently revised its capital rules to require FSLIC-insured institutions to increase their capital from a minimum of 3% to a maximum of 6% over a period estimated to be from 6 to 12 years, 12 C.F.R. § 563.13, the opportunity to make interstate acquisitions may increase to the extent thrifts experience difficulty in meeting these new standards.

thrifts are not as constrained as bank holding companies because they are required to only maintain the largest portion of their deposits in a state within the region while bank holding companies must maintain at least 75% of their deposits in the region. Theoretically, a Pennsylvania thrift could make acquisitions in Oregon (assuming Oregon permits entry) and collect significant deposits in that state, yet still expand within the region if its largest concentration of deposits is located in a state within the region. Conversely, after March 4, 1990, bank holding companies within the region will not be constrained by any deposit concentration rules but thrifts within the region will still be subject to the requirement that the largest concentration of deposits must be located in a state within the region.

IV. THE FHLBB'S INTERSTATE REGULATION

1. *Basic Authority.*

The ability of a federal thrift (mutual or stock) institution to expand interstate is a recent development. On April 24, 1986, the FHLBB adopted a regulation[76] which provides for (i) general equality between federal thrifts and state-chartered thrifts with respect to interstate expansion rights, and (ii) broader rights for federal thrifts acquiring a failing institution. The rules with respect to the acquisition of failing thrifts are different from the rules applicable to the acquisition of healthy thrifts and are quite a good deal more liberal.

In nonsupervisory cases (i.e., transactions involving financially healthy institutions not receiving FSLIC assistance or subject to any regulatory order), the regulation provides that a member of the Federal Home Loan Bank System and any institution insured by the Federal Savings and Loan Insurance Corporation may operate a branch office in a state other than the state in which its home office is located if the law of the state in which the federal thrift is located *and* the law of the state in which the branch is to be located both would permit the establishment of such a branch if the federal thrift were a state-chartered institution chartered by the federal thrift's home state.

Of particular significance is that the point of reference for determining whether a given federal thrift has interstate branching rights is the interstate rights of state-chartered thrifts in the home state of the federal thrift and not the rights of *all* state-chartered financial institutions. In some states this places federal thrifts at a disadvantage *vis a vis* national banks and bank holding companies because many states have enacted legislation that permits interstate expansion by bank holding companies but have not yet enacted interstate thrift legislation. For example, in the states which comprise the region defined in Pennsylvania's bills, Kentucky has passed interstate bank legislation but has not, as yet, enacted similar legislation for thrifts. Thus, an out-of-state bank holding company can enter this jurisdiction to acquire a bank or bank holding company but a federal thrift cannot enter to acquire a thrift. The FHLBB has taken note of this in the commentary accompanying the

---

76. 12 C.F.R § 556.5. See Exhibit "D."

final regulation, but the Board stated that it believed a conservative approach to interstate expansion is appropriate, at least initially.[77]

A further hindrance to interstate expansion is the fact that the new regulation requires that both the home state of the federal thrift and the state which it seeks to enter permit interstate expansion. The Douglas amendment to the BHCA requires only that the home state of the acquiree permit ownership by out-of-state bank holding companies. Thus, a bank holding company can enter a state which permits ownership of banks by out-of-state entities without reciprocity regardless of the enactment of interstate legislation in the acquiror's home state. A federally-chartered thrift, however, could not branch into any state that permits ownership of thrifts by out-of-state entities without reciprocity until the law of the acquiror's home state permitted state-chartered thrifts to branch interstate.

Although the basic authority of a federal thrift to expand across state borders is determined by reference to state law, the regulation specifies that a federal thrift need not obtain any state approval or meet any other state prerequisite. Thus, under the federal regulation whether a federal thrift can merge, make acquisitions or establish *de novo* branches is determined by state law (as construed by the FHLBB) but a federal thrift need not meet any investment standards, deposit concentration guidelines or other state criteria. This is in direct conflict with Pennsylvania legislation. The Pennsylvania bills require approval of the DOB before any regional association or regional savings bank enters Pennsylvania and before any Pennsylvania association or savings banks expands into another state. Because the definitions of regional association, regional savings bank, Pennsylvania association and Pennsylvania savings bank all include the corresponding federal thrift institutions, the legislation purports to give the DOB approval over transactions which the federal regulation specifically states requires no state approval. In addition to the state approval requirement which by itself conflicts with the regulation, the DOB is instructed to consider the availability of basic credit and transaction account services before approving any interstate transaction. This too conflicts with the federal regulation because it purports to set investment and operational standards for federal thrifts. Nothing in the legislative history of the thrift bills indicates that these conflicts were addressed or even recognized. No test of this apparent conflict has yet arisen and thrifts will probably seek both sets of approvals. However, if the Pennsylvania approval process were tested, the provisions of the federal regulation would probably prevail under federal preemption principles.

Although state law may permit a thrift to merge, make acquisitions or establish branches across state lines, the federal regulation clearly makes any interstate transaction subject to the provisions of the SLHCA. As noted, except in supervisory cases,[78] a savings and loan holding company cannot control an FSLIC or FDIC-insured institution in more than one state. In order to preserve observance of this statutory prohibition, the regulation specifically states that it does not authorize a

---

77. 51 F.R. p. 16504. See Exhibit "D."
78. A supervisory case is a transaction involving a financially unstable institution in which the FSLIC provides financial assistance or arranges the transaction.

federal thrift to become a savings and loan holding company controlling an insured institution in a state other than the state of its home office.[79] Accordingly, a Pennsylvania thrift cannot acquire an Ohio thrift and operate it as a subsidiary even if the legislation of both states would permit such an acquisition because the Pennsylvania thrift would then control a thrift in another state. The only alternative for interstate transactions between institutions is merger. When two institutions merge, the resulting entity is just one institution and no violation of the SLHCA results even though it would conduct operations in more than one state. This rule, which is so markedly different from the rules for commercial banks, could have a chilling effect on interstate transactions because an acquiror cannot offer an acquiree located in another state an opportunity to retain autonomy. The acquiree could still be operated as a separate division of the acquiror but it cannot maintain a separate corporate identity.

2. *Basic Interstate Rules.*

The FHLBB regulation also establishes a number of rules regarding the order in which thrifts within a holding company can branch interstate. The net result of these rules is to permit only one *federal* thrift in any holding company structure to exercise interstate rights. An unlimited number of state thrifts can expand interstate subject only to the restrictions of applicable state law and the SLHCA. The rules can be summarized as follows:

Rule 1. If a federal thrift is an ultimate savings and loan holding company (i.e. the parent which is not controlled by any other company) and no *state-chartered,* insured institution within the holding company structure (i.e. wholly-owned by the parent) has exercised interstate rights, then the parent holding company is the only *federal* thrift in the holding company structure that can exercise interstate rights under the regulation.

Rule 2. A federal thrift which is a holding company cannot exercise interstate rights if any other *insured institution,* whether state or federally-chartered, in the holding company structure has exercised its interstate rights.

Rule 3. A federal thrift which is a subsidiary of an insured institution cannot exercise its interstate rights if any other *insured institution* in the holding company structure has exercised its interstate rights.

Rule 4. A federal thrift which has exercised its interstate rights must divest its interstate operation if another *insured institution* in its holding company structure exercises its interstate rights.

It is important to note that the regulation only applies to interstate expansion of *federal thrifts* in a holding company structure. The power of state-chartered thrifts in holding company structures to expand interstate is governed by state law and the SLHCA. A few examples can best illustrate the possible permutations that arise out of these rules. In each example assume all thrifts have their home offices in the same state.

---

79. An institution's home office is determined as of the later of its charter date or December 20, 1985. Relocation is permitted if the institution demonstrates that the change of home office is not designed principally to obtain branching advantages. 12 C.F.R. 556.5(a)(3)(1). See Exhibit "D".

Example 1
Assume the following structure:

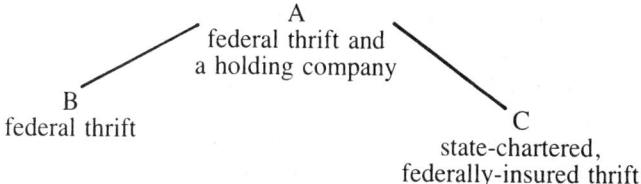

a. If neither A, B or C has exercised its interstate rights then A is the only federal thrift which can exercise interstate rights pursuant to Rule 1 above. C also may have interstate rights under state law which are not constrained by the SLHCA. However, if A exercises its interstate rights and C subsequently does so A would have to divest its interstate operations under Rule 4.

b. If B exercises its interstate rights then A cannot expand interstate under Rule 2, but again, C may have rights under state law which are not constrained by the SLHCA. If C exercises these rights, B must divest under Rule 4.

c. If C expands interstate, neither A or B can do so under Rules 2 and 3.

Example 2
Assume the following structure:

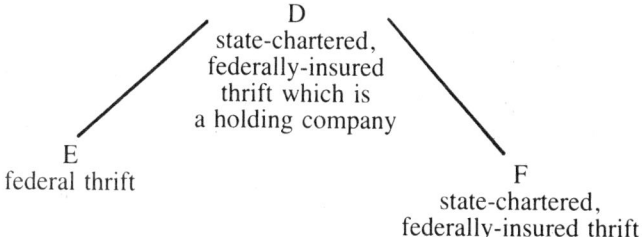

a. If D expands interstate, E may not do so under Rule 3 but F may under applicable state law.

b. If F expands interstate, E may not do so under Rule 3 but D may under applicable state law.

c. If E expands interstate, D and F may still have interstate rights. If either D or F exercises these rights, E must divest its interstate operation under Rule 4.

Example 3
Assume the following structure:

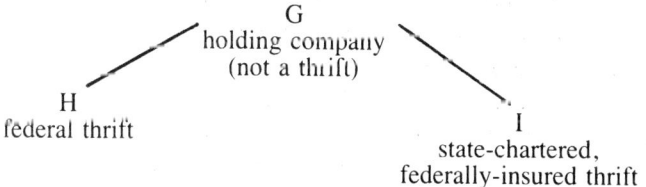

a. G cannot acquire a thrift in another state under the SLHCA.

b. If H expands interstate, I may still expand interstate (by branching or merger) but then H would be forced to divest under Rule 4.

c. If I expands interstate, H may not do so under Rule 4.

Because the regulation reaches only federal thrifts, greater flexibility in interstate branching is available to state thrifts in a holding company. For example, assume a holding company controls a federal thrift in Philadelphia and a state thrift in Pittsburgh. If the Pittsburgh-based state thrift establishes a *de novo* branch in Ohio, the Philadelphia federal thrift cannot expand interstate. However, if the federal thrift in Philadelphia were a state thrift it could branch into New Jersey (if New Jersey law permitted) even though its Pittsburgh affiliate had entered Ohio. This result may encourage the conversion of federal thrifts to state charters and the chartering of new state thrifts.

The regulation concerning branching establishes special rules for federal associations that are part of an existing multi-state savings and loan holding company. Multi-state holding companies exist either because they were formed prior to passage of the SLHCA in 1967 or because they arose as a result of an emergency acquisition approved by the Bank Board under its general supervisory authority or under the Garn-St. Germain Depository Institutions Act of 1982 (the "DIA"). The purpose of the special rules for federal associations in multi-state holding companies is to prevent the use of these existing multi-state structures and the new regulation as a basis to "leverage" wide ranging branching authority. These rules can be summarized as follows:

> 1. A federal thrift which is part of a multi-state holding company cannot exercise its interstate rights if any other subsidiary insured institution in its holding company has exercised its interstate rights.

> 2. A federal thrift cannot exercise its interstate rights if it is not located in the state designated by its parent pursuant to the SLHCA[80] as its home state.

> 3. A federal thrift may not exercise any interstate rights if it was acquired by an existing holding company under the DIA and no other subsidiary of the holding company that either (i) is located in the holding company's designated home state, or (ii) existed prior to the acquisition of the federal thrift under the DIA possesses interstate rights.

3. *Interstate Expansion In Supervisory Cases.*

In addition to the limited interstate branching rights granted to federal thrifts, the new regulation potentially grants very broad rights to federal thrifts which acquire failed or failing thrifts. Because of the large number of thrifts that are experiencing severe financial difficulty, this exception may swallow the rule. The eventual national result could be that a number of large thrifts that make supervisory acquisitions could acquire essentially national branching rights.

---

80. 12 U.S.C. §1730a(e)(3)(B). See Exhibit "H".

In order to encourage the acquisition of failed or failing thrifts, the FHLBB will permit the acquiror, as part of its application to acquire the troubled target, to also apply for broader interstate rights. Under the rule, an applicant can request branching rights in the greater of (i) three states in addition to the state or states in which the target institution operates, or (ii) if the target's home office is located in a state that has enacted regional interstate legislation, then the states within the regional compact. Once, an acquiror has entered a state pursuant to this provision, further branching within the state will be permitted without regard to the branching rules established for nonsupervisory transactions.

The regulation specifies certain criteria and preferences that the Bank Board will use in evaluating applications to acquire a failed or failing thrift. First, the regulation provides that no application shall be approved unless the Board finds that (i) the branching authority sought is reasonably related to the office structure of the applicant before or *after* the acquisition of the target, and (ii) the acquisition will be of very substantial benefit to the FSLIC "in a measure sufficient to constitute a compelling factor in determining to make an award to the applicant."[81] What showing will have to be made to convince the Bank Board that the requested branching rights are reasonably related to the office structure of the applicant remains to be seen, but the fact that this showing can be made on the basis of the applicant's office structure after the acquisition suggests that the standard will not be high. For example, First Nationwide of San Francisco, which acquired failed thrifts in Ohio, requested and received branching rights in Pennsylvania and Colorado. Clearly, the standard will vary depending upon the severity of the financial condition of the institution the Bank Board is attempting to sell and the number of interested suitors.

The regulation also states that, in connection with supervisory merger applications, preference will be given to (i) those applicants that seek limited branching authority over those seeking broader authority, and (ii) those applicants seeking branching rights within a regional compact or contiguous states over those seeking more geographically dispersed branching authority. Again, while these may be the expressed preferences of the Board, the First Nationwide example cited above indicates that they are not rigid rules.

The branching rules for supervisory transactions also apply to reverse mergers in which the target is the surviving entity and in transactions in which failed or failing insured institution subsidiaries of other companies are acquired.

---

81. 12 C.F.R. §556.5(a)(3)(ii)(b)(2). See Exhibit "D."

The broad scope of the interstate branching rules in supervisory transactions presents a significant opportunity for well-capitalized thrifts and thrifts that have access to the capital markets because they can afford to pay the price to enter a new state either through existing resources or by raising new capital. This will clearly favor stock institutions over mutual institutions because of their greater ability to raise capital. Furthermore, the rules will almost certainly create a number of institutions with national or large regional branching rights. Thus, although Pennsylvania's interstate thrift legislation does not contain a national trigger, Pennsylvania institutions may well face national competition even before commercial banks do.

4. *Interstate Rights for Thrifts Under Pennsylvania and Federal Law.*

As noted, the Pennsylvania legislation would permit thrifts to expand interstate through *de novo* branching, merger or acquisition. The provisions of the SLHCA, however, place restrictions on these otherwise unfettered rights because of the prohibition against a savings and loan holding company controlling thrifts in more than one state. The following is a chart of the permissible interstate activity for thrifts under Pennsylvania and federal law:

	Permissible Activity		
	Branching[82]	**Merger**	**Acquisition[83]**
State Thrift	Yes	Yes[84]	No
Federal Thrift	Yes	Yes[85]	No
Thrift Holding Company that is an insured institution	Yes	Yes[86]	No
Thrift Subsidiary of Thrift Holding Company	Yes	Yes[87]	No
Thrift Holding Company (not an insured institution)	N/A	No[88]	No

V. THE LEGISLATION OF OTHER STATES IN THE REGION

Discussed below are the various statutes of states within the region defined by Pennsylvania's bills which concern interstate bank and thrift expansion.

Delaware. On May 14, 1987, Delaware enacted interstate banking legislation.[89] The legislation provides that on or after January 1, 1988 but before June 30, 1990, bank holding companies located in Maryland, New Jersey, Pennsylvania, Ohio, Virginia or the District of Columbia may acquire a Delaware bank or bank holding company, provided the home state of the acquiror has enacted reciprocal legislation. After June 30, 1990, a national trigger takes effect. The only significant

---

82. Under the Pennsylvania legislation and the federal interstate regulation any thrift, including a thrift which is itself a holding company, can branch interstate. Federal thrifts, however, are subject to the restriction that only one federal thrift in a holding company can exercise interstate rights.

83. In general, interstate acquisitions violate the SLHCA because of the prohibition against controlling thrifts in more than one state. Theoretically, it would be possible for a thrift to make *one* interstate acquisition and operate the acquiree as a subsidiary. This transaction would make the acquiror a holding company but it would control only one other insured institution, albeit in another state. However, the interstate regulation specifically states that it does not authorize a thrift to become a holding company controlling a thrift in another state. Although the regulation does not authorize such a transaction, neither does it prohibit it, nor, by its strict terms, does the SLHCA. Thus, the FHLBB's policy on this type of transaction is not entirely clear. Some transactions such as the one described have been approved but the acquiror has also acquired a failed or failing thrift in the other state as part of the transaction. Considerable doubt exists as to whether a transaction not involving the acquisition of both a healthy and failing thrift would be approved.

84. Pennsylvania's legislation permits interstate mergers.

85. The FHLBB regulations permit interstate mergers between insured institutions if state law would permit the transaction.

86. Pennsylvania and FHLBB regulations permit mergers by thrifts that are also holding companies except that a federal thrift that is an ultimate thrift holding company cannot exercise interstate rights if another thrift in the holding company structure has exercised such rights.

87. A subsidiary of a thrift holding company can merge interstate except that a federal thrift subsidiary can do so only if no other thrift in the holding company structure has exercised interstate rights.

88. A holding company cannot merge with a holding company that controls a thrift in another state because the result would be a holding company controlling thrifts in more than one state and this would violate the SLHCA.

89. Del. Code Ann. tit. 5, §841 *et seq.* (1987).

legislation provides that the shareholders of any Delaware bank or bank holding company, by majority vote, may elect to be exempt from the interstate legislation. Delaware has also enacted identical legislation regarding savings banks except that the list of potential acquirors includes state- and federally-chartered savings banks and savings and loan associations, as well as savings and loan holding companies.[90] Obviously, this is because of the limitations imposed by the SLHCA.

One week after enactment, the Delaware legislation was utilized when Reading, Pennsylvania-based Meridian Bancorp, Inc. announced its acquisition of Wilmington-based Delaware Trust Company in a transaction valued at approximately $196 million.

Kentucky. Kentucky enacted interstate banking legislation that became effective on July 13, 1984.[91] Initially, only bank or bank holding companies located in states contiguous to Kentucky which had passed reciprocal legislation could acquire a Kentucky bank or bank holding company. On July 13, 1986, Kentucky's national trigger took effect and now a bank or bank holding company located in any state can acquire a Kentucky bank or bank holding company provided the state in which the acquiror is located has passed reciprocal legislation which would permit Kentucky bank holding companies to enter that state.

The Kentucky legislation contains only two restrictions which apply to both intrastate and interstate acquisitions. First, no bank or bank holding company may acquire control of a bank or bank holding company if the acquisition would give the acquiror more than 15% of all deposits in Kentucky banks. Second, until July 13, 1989, no individual or company may acquire more than three banks in any twelve month period, provided, however, that one acquisition of a bank holding company which has in excess of three bank subsidiaries is permitted. The banks in excess of three would be counted against future acquisitions within the five year period. Thus, a bank holding company which acquires a Kentucky bank holding company which has six banking subsidiaries could not make another acquisition in Kentucky for two years. Because these provisions are applicable both to Kentucky and out-of-state bank holding companies, Kentucky's legislation should be reciprocal with Pennsylvania's legislation. Kentucky has not enacted interstate thrift legislation.

One interstate transaction between a Pennsylvania and Kentucky banking organization has been announced, the acquisition of Louisville, Kentucky-based Citizens Fidelity Corp. by Pittsburgh, Pennsylvania-based PNC Financial Corp.

Maryland. Maryland enacted interstate banking legislation which became effective on July 1, 1985.[92] Initially, the legislation permits the acquisition of Maryland banks and bank holding companies by other bank holding companies located in Delaware, Virginia, West Virginia and the District of Columbia provided these states extend reciprocity to Maryland bank holding companies. On July 1,

---
90. Del. Code Ann. tit. 5, §831 *et seq.* (1987)
91. 12 Ky. Rev. Stat. § 287.900 (1984).
92. Md. Fin. Inst. Code Ann. §§ 5-1001 through 5-1007.

1987, bank holding companies located in eleven other states, including Pennsylvania, can acquire Maryland institutions if their home states have adopted reciprocal legislation.

The Maryland legislation contains two important restrictions. First, no out-of-state bank holding company may acquire a Maryland bank or bank holding company whose subsidiary bank has been in operation for less than four years. Second, as part of the approval process of any acquisition by an out-of-state bank holding company, the Maryland Banking Commissioner is required to assess the amount and cost of consumer services to be offered, the steps to be taken to meet the credit needs of small businesses and individuals, and the past record of the acquiror in meeting these credit needs in its home state. This consumer protection aspect of the legislation is very similar to the provisions contained in Pennsylvania's interstate laws and because there are no other conflicts, the interstate laws of Pennsylvania and Maryland should be reciprocal.

The Maryland legislation does not contain a national trigger. The Maryland legislation would permit entry by bank holding companies from only six of the eight states which can enter Pennsylvania. New Jersey and Ohio are excluded. Conversely, until 1990 when Pennsylvania's national trigger takes effect, only bank holding companies from five of the other fourteen states that can enter Maryland can enter Pennsylvania. They are Delaware, Kentucky, Virginia, West Virginia and the District of Columbia.

In April 1987, Maryland enacted interstate legislation for thrifts which on or after July 1, 1987, permits thrifts and thrift holding companies located in the same 15 state region defined by Maryland's banking bill to acquire a Maryland thrift or thrift holding company provided the acquiror's home state has enacted reciprocal legislation. Interstate branching is not permitted.

New Jersey. On March 28, 1986, New Jersey adopted interstate legislation.[93] This legislation permits bank holding companies located in 14 states, including Pennsylvania, to acquire a New Jersey bank or bank holding company provided the home state of such institution has adopted reciprocal legislation. A national trigger takes effect when at least thirteen states, at least four of which are among the ten states with the largest amount of commercial bank deposits, have reciprocal legislation. All bank holding companies that are located in states from which they can enter Pennsylvania, can also enter New Jersey. Conversely, until Pennsylvania's national trigger takes effect, only bank holding companies located in six of the states that can enter New Jersey also can enter Pennsylvania.

The New Jersey legislation requires that any acquiror have at least 75% of its deposits located within the defined region and 50% of such deposits in states in that region that have passed reciprocal legislation. The legislation also prohibits any acquisition that would result in the acquiror owning stock in institutions that control more than 12% percent of the total deposits of all New Jersey depository institutions. (This percentage is scheduled to increase to 13.5%). The interstate laws of Pennsylvania and New Jersey are reciprocal.

Three interstate transactions between Pennsylvania and New Jersey banking organizations have been announced: the Midlantic Corporation acquisition of Continental Bancorp, Inc., the CoreStates Financial Corp. acquisition of New Jersey

---

93. N.J. Rev. Stat. § 17:9A-1 et seq. (1986).

National Corp. and the Commerce Bancorp, Inc. acquisition of Commerce Bank/Pennsylvania, N.A.

On June 4, 1987, the New Jersey legislature enacted interstate legislation for thrifts which is essentially a mirror image of the New Jersey banking legislation. The bill applies to both thrifts and thrift holding companies. Interstate branching is not permitted. At this writing Governor Kean had not yet signed the bill but was expected to do so. It will become effective immediately upon signature.

Ohio. Ohio enacted interstate legislation for both banks and thrifts in 1985.[94] Under the legislation a bank holding company located in any state contiguous to Ohio (including, of course, Pennsylvania) or Delaware, the District of Columbia, Illinois, Maryland, Missouri, New Jersey, Tennessee, Virginia or Wisconsin may acquire an Ohio bank or bank holding company provided reciprocity exists. Similarly, a savings and loan association or savings and loan holding company located in the aforementioned states can acquire an Ohio state-chartered savings and loan association or Ohio savings and loan holding company if reciprocity exists. Both the banking and thrift legislation have a three year national trigger. Accordingly, in 1988 Ohio will be open to nationwide reciprocal expansion of banks and thrifts.

The Ohio legislation contains two important restrictions. First, no acquisition will be permitted if the resulting institution will control more than 20% of the deposits of all Ohio financial institutions. Second, any acquisition must be approved by two-thirds of the shareholders of the Ohio institution. This approval requirement can be altered by the shareholders if they choose to do so. Finally, any acquiror of an Ohio institution subjects itself to examination by Ohio regulators. The interstate laws of Pennsylvania and Ohio appear to be reciprocal.

Virginia. Virginia enacted interstate banking and thrift legislation in 1985.[95] Under the legislation a bank holding company located within the prescribed region may acquire a state or national bank or a bank holding company located in Virginia, provided reciprocity exists. Also, a thrift or thrift holding company located in the prescribed region may acquire a state or federally-chartered thrift located in Virginia if reciprocity exists. The prescribed region includes Alabama, Arkansas, Florida, Georgia, Kentucky, Louisiana, Maryland, Mississippi, North Carolina, South Carolina, Tennessee, Virginia, West Virginia and the District of Columbia. The region does not include Pennsylvania, and, in fact, the only states which are in Virginia's region which are also in Pennsylvania's are West Virginia, the District of Columbia and Virginia itself. Moreover, the Virginia legislation does not contain a national trigger. Accordingly, Virginia's legislation is not reciprocal with Pennsylvania's and therefore at the present time no Pennsylvania institution can expand into Virginia absent a supervisory merger or acquisition effected pursuant to the DIA or otherwise. Under the FHLBB's interstate regulation, federally-chartered thrifts located in Virginia may branch into the District of Columbia.

West Virginia. West Virginia adopted interstate banking and thrift legislation on February 28, 1986.[96] The legislation provides that after December 31, 1987, a bank holding company located anywhere in the United States may acquire a West

---

94. Ohio Rev. Code Ann. § 1151.71.
95. Va. Code §§ 6.1-194 and 6.1-398 et seq.
96. W. Va. Code §§ 31-6-7a and 31A-8A-7.

Virginia bank or bank holding company provided the acquiror's home state has enacted reciprocal legislation. Similarly, after December 31, 1987, any thrift or thrift holding company may acquire a West Virginia building and loan association provided reciprocity exists. The West Virginia statute covers both state and national banks but only state-chartered building and loan associations.

The West Virginia legislation contains three significant restrictions. First, no acquisition of any West Virginia institution will be permitted that has been in existence for less than two years. Second, no acquisition will be permitted that results in the acquiror attaining control of 20% of the total deposits held by all financial institutions located in West Virginia. Finally, the shareholders of a West Virginia bank, bank holding company or state-chartered building and loan association must approve an acquisition by an out-of-state institution by a two-thirds vote. The shareholders can alter this requirement by amendment of their articles if they choose to do so. The Pennsylvania and West Virginia laws appear to be reciprocal.

District of Columbia. The District of Columbia enacted interstate banking legislation in 1985.[97] Under the legislation a bank holding company located in a prescribed region may acquire a District of Columbia bank or bank holding company if reciprocity exists. The prescribed region includes the District of Columbia, Alabama, Florida, Georgia, Louisiana, Maryland, Mississippi, North Carolina, South Carolina, Tennessee, Virginia and West Virginia. Pennsylvania is not included within the region and the legislation contains no national trigger. Therefore, the Pennsylvania and District of Columbia laws are not reciprocal.

All thrifts in the District of Columbia are federally-chartered and are governed by the FHLBB's interstate branching regulation. Under that regulation, in addition to other rights they may have, District of Columbia thrifts can branch into either Maryland or Virginia, but not both.

VI. IMPACT OF INTERSTATE LEGISLATION

The new legislation in Pennsylvania and other states, together with the new regulatory stance of the FHLBB, is certain to spur great changes in the financial services industry. Consolidation is inevitable but questions concerning the results of this consolidation await answers. Will consolidation enhance or inhibit competition? Will consolidation cause a net outflow of deposits from certain geographic areas? Will small institutions survive? What choices face the management of financial institutions? What strategies will help management reach their goals? Will Pennsylvania be a net "winner" in the coming interstate consolidation? What will be the particular consequences on banks, thrifts, banks and thrifts *vis a vis* each other and banks and thrifts *vis a vis* other financial institution competitors? This section of the article will suggest some possible answers to these questions. No attempt has been made to predict the effect that the erosion of barriers in the international financial and capital markets and the ascendancy of foreign financial institutions will have on the domestic financial services industry. This is because significant data is not yet available. However, foreign competition is increasing, can be expected to continue and may significantly affect the domestic market in the future.

---

97. D.C. Code Ann. §§ 26-801 through 26-809.

A. The Effect on Competition.

Perhaps the greatest fear expressed by opponents of interstate banking is that the end result will be oligopoly. It is argued that only a few large banks will survive the consolidation and possess sufficient market strength to set prices and strangle competition. Opponents fear that access of the poor and middle class to reasonably priced credit and transaction account services will be adversely affected.

This was not the intent of interstate banking legislation. Although the financial services industry in Pennsylvania probably will be dominated by a small number of "super regionals" with respect to deposit volume, and to a lesser extent, with respect to loan volume, small institutions may very well survive and indeed flourish. Moreover, a predatory oligopoly is not necessarily the natural consequence of the dominance of super regionals.

1. *Regional Effects.*

There seems to be little doubt that interstate legislation will increase the concentration of the banking and thrift industry on a regional level.[98] Although little empirical evidence of this conclusion is yet available, an examination of the concentration levels in states which permit state-wide banking compared to states which limit expansion demonstrates the following. As of March 1985, states that permitted state-wide branching of banks had an average five-firm deposit concentration ratio of 72.4%. By contrast, unit banking states in which multi-bank holding companies controlled over half of the deposits had an average concentration ratio of 49%, while unit banking states where less than half of the deposits are controlled by multi-bank holding companies had an average concentration ratio of only 31.6%.[99] It can be inferred from this data that the same result will occur on the regional level during the initial interstate consolidation. With respect to commercial banks, the removal of the regional boundary in Pennsylvania in 1990 and therefore the significant increase in the potential entrants into the regional market may temporarily slow or reverse this consolidation trend in the short term, but eventually regional consolidation seems likely to occur.

2. *National Effects.*

Although regional compacts will almost certainly increase concentration at the regional level, the impact of such legislation on national concentration is less clear. Whether national concentration occurs will depend in large measure on the acquisition targets chosen by nonregional entrants. An argument can be made that the growth of regional compacts will actually reduce national banking concentration

---

98. *See generally,* S. Rhoades, *Concentration in Local and National Markets,* Economic Review, Federal Reserve Bank of Atlanta, Interstate Banking Laws — Time to Remodel? at p. 28 (hereinafter, S. Rhoades) for a general discussion of the effect of interstate banking on consolidation at the local, regional and national level.

99. S. Rhoades, *supra* Note 98, at p. 29. Emphasis on deposit concentration ratios among banks overlooks the effects of disintermediation and competition for deposits from other financial services firms such as insurance companies and brokerage houses. In addition, analysis of deposit concentrations addresses only the liability side of the balance sheet. On the asset side, as banks grow they tend to provide more services over a greater geographic area including the international market. Similarly, thrifts which grow often tend to take on the characteristics of banks. Thus, in general conclusions about competition which are based solely on deposit ratios may underestimate the degree of competition in the financial services industry.

levels over the short term and preserve regional competition. A frequently used measure of banking concentration is the Herfindahl Index which reflects both the total number of banking organizations in the industry and their size distribution. The national Herfindahl Index increases when banking organizations merge as well as when the top tier of banking organizations (which includes only the very largest money center banks) grow more quickly than the industry as a whole. Conversely, the index decreases as new banks are formed or if banking organizations that are smaller than the top money center banks grow internally faster than the industry.[100] Although regional mergers increase the concentration index, if large regional organizations grow internally more quickly than the money center banks, the index decreases. The barrier imposed by regional compacts will insulate the large regionals from money center bank competition and perhaps enhance their ability to grow internally. The performance of the banking industry recently suggests that this may in fact be occurring. The large super regionals have consistently out-performed the New York money center banks. Return on assets for the large regionals is on average far superior to the return on assets of money center banks.[101]

The superior performance of the super regionals has been reflected in their market capitalization. In some instances, the market capitalization of the super regionals has exceeded the market capitalization of much larger institutions. The result may be that these super regionals could be virtually immune to takeover by many money center banks because the cost, in terms of dilution, would be unacceptable to the acquiror's existing shareholders. Accordingly, those money center banks that choose to expand nationally may be forced to acquire smaller institutions or thrifts.[102] The result could be decreased concentration and enhanced competition within a region.

100. Dunham, C., and Syron, R., *Interstate Banking: The Drive to Consolidate*, New England Economic Review, May/June 1984 (hereinafter Dunham and Syron).

101. American Banker, September 30, 1986 at p. 1, col. 1.

102. In general bank holding companies cannot acquire thrifts because bank holding companies can only acquire "banks" within the meaning of the BHCA and thrifts are expressly excluded from the definition of "banks" under the BHCA. However, a number of thrifts have been acquired by bank holding companies. In such transactions, the acquiree thrift immediately converts its charter to a national bank charter, converts its federal insurance from FSLIC to FDIC and takes demand deposits. The FHLBB is seeking to discourage this practice because it is concerned that healthy FSLIC-insured thrifts will be acquired and thus leave the already financially troubled FSLIC with only financially weak thrifts. Recently the FSLIC has charged "exit fees" and the FHLBB has taken the position that termination of FSLIC insurance constitutes a liquidation which requires recently converted thrifts to pay its former mutual depositors the amount contained in the "liquidation account" which is required to be established upon conversion. (At this writing, Barnett Bank in Florida, which is in the process of acquiring a thrift, is challenging the imposition of the exit fee by the FSLIC and has won a temporary injunction against the imposition of an exit fee by the FSLIC.) In addition, a number of other practical barriers exist. For tax purposes, the acquisition of a thrift by a bank may cause recognition of the thrift's bad debt reserve as income. In addition, the accounting profession generally requires banks to have greater reserves for loan losses than thrifts. This may require the thrift to increase its provision for loan loss and thereby decrease net income. Failing thrifts have also been acquired by bank holding companies under the DIA. In some of these cases the acquiree retains its status as a thrift but the Federal Reserve Board enforces a strict separation of operations between the thrift and the bank holding company's banking subsidiaries. In Pennsylvania, a thrift that wants to be acquired by a bank holding company can become a state-chartered savings bank and take demand deposits and make commercial loans. As such, it meets the definition of bank under the BHCA and conversion to a national charter is not necessary to effect the transaction.

Thus, it can be argued that the short-term effect of regional compact legislation will decrease national banking concentration. However, if one accepts the conclusion that regional concentration will increase due to regional pacts just as state-wide concentration increases when full state-wide expansion is permitted, then as regional compacts dissolve and full interstate banking becomes a reality, one should also conclude that nationwide banking concentration will increase.

The existence of interstate banking legislation does not mean that the degree of national concentration of banking resources will become excessive. The composition of the United States market and existing regulatory and legislative framework may prevent undue concentration.[103]

The factors often cited as important in determining concentration include (i) the size of the market, (ii) barriers to entry such as interstate restrictions and capital requirements, (iii) merger policy including both interstate restrictions and antitrust legislation, (iv) control of the payments system, and (v) product line restriction.[104] The size of the United States banking market is enormous. There are over 14,000 banking organizations and 4,000 to 5,000 thrift institutions in the United States. This fact alone suggests that significant increased national concentration, while inevitable, will not happen overnight and may not reach pernicious levels.[105]

Clearly, one of the most important entry barriers in the United States banking industry has been the inability to expand interstate or intrastate although many intrastate barriers have now eroded. Unrestricted geographic expansion rights tend to increase concentration but this may be mitigated by competition from nonbank entities and the entry of *de novo* institutions.[106] To the extent both U.S. banks and thrifts are permitted to expand geographically, concentration will increase. However, competition from nonbanking firms is definitely on the increase and, except for regulatory capital requirements, no significant restrictions exist on the establishment of *de novo* institutions.

A liberal merger policy also generally contributes to concentration. Without interstate restrictions, United States bank merger policy would be in large measure a function of the antitrust laws. The antitrust laws effectively promote banking and thrift competition at the local level but as yet have not been tested at the national level. To date, the antitrust analysis undertaken by the Federal Reserve Board in

---

103. Support for this assertion can be found by examining the concentration levels of other industrial countries with nationwide branching. The five-firm demand deposit concentration ratio for the Canadian wholesale banking market is 85% yet the ratio for the Japanese market (wholesale and retail) is only 22%. The current United States concentration ratio is approximately 19%. This suggests that significant competition can exist even if full interstate banking becomes a reality. H. Baer and L. Mote, *The Effect of Nationwide Banking on Concentration: Evidence from Abroad*, p. 14. Economic Perspectives, Federal Reserve Bank of Chicago, January/February 1985 (hereinafter Baer and Mote).
104. Baer and Mote, *supra* Note 103. Messrs. Baer and Mote found similar factors to be important determinants of banking concentration in Canada, France, Great Britain, Japan and West Germany.
105. *See generally*, Danielson, "Interstate Banking: Competitive Threat or Minor Transformation," Banking Expansion Reporter, Vol. 4, No. 3, February 4, 1985.
106. *See generally*, S. Rhoades, *supra* Note 98.

connection with merger and acquisition transactions has focused on the concentration of resources within a given Standard Metropolitan Statistical Area (SMSA). As interstate expansion proceeds, the relevant geographic market will almost certainly have to be redefined to include a larger area.[107] Moreover, as competition increases from nonbank financial institutions and the range of products expands, the relevant product market may have to be redefined.

As the degree of control over the payments system increases, concentration also increases. In the United Kingdom, a very few number of institutions control the clearing of checks and other payments.[108] In the United States this function is principally performed by the Federal Reserve Banks. Because this function is performed by a neutral independent agency, no competitive barriers should exist and therefore this should not cause banking concentration.

Finally, restrictions on product lines tend to increase concentration. With respect to product line diversification, commercial banks have wide banking powers in the United States. Their ability to expand into other financial markets such as the underwriting of securities is restricted, however.[109] Thrifts are subject to product line restrictions (thrifts, however, can engage in certain activities, such as direct equity investment in real estate, which banks cannot do). Although these restrictions were liberalized by the DIA in 1982, federal thrifts still can only make commercial loans up to 10% of their assets and consumer loans up to 30% of their assets and therefore they are not on an equal footing with commercial banks.[110] To the degree that thrift powers are liberalized in the future, or the capital level of the thrift industry is raised, competition between banks and thrifts will increase and concentration will decrease.[111]

In sum, in the United States, a number of factors militate against the rise of a banking oligopoly. Both the size of the geographic market and the number of existing competitors is quite large. Competition from nonbank firms is vigorous and rising. No interested party has control over any significant banking function such as the payment system, and finally, if antitrust analysis is refined in light of changing conditions, the existing antitrust laws should effectively prevent undue concentration at both the regional and national level, much as they currently do at the local level.

3. *Local Effects.*

Even if it is assumed that interstate banking and thrift legislation will increase concentration at both the regional and national levels, such legislation probably will

---

107. At least one commentator has suggested that Congress enact deposit concentration limits similar to those contained in some state interstate bills. *See* Dunham and Syron, *supra* Note 100, at 25.
108. Baer and Mote, supra Note 103, at p. 5.
109. The Glass-Steagall Act prohibits banks from underwriting most securities, 12 U.S.C. §§ 24, 78, 377 and 378. Because of the ability to establish nonbank banks, however, other financial institutions are encroaching on the traditional product lines of banks.
110. 12 U.S.C. § 1464.
111. Although thrifts are subject to significant product line restrictions, unitary thrift holding companies (i.e. only one insured institution subsidiary) have virtually no restrictions on their powers and therefore may be able to compete effectively with banks through the holding company structure.

have little or no adverse effect on competition within an SMSA. Support for this assertion can be found by comparing the deposit concentration in SMSAs located in state-wide branching jurisdictions and with those SMSAs in more restrictive jurisdictions. In general, the differences are slight. For states that permit unlimited statewide branching, the average SMSA concentration is 73.4%. For states with limited branching in which multi-bank holding companies (MBHCs) control more than half the deposits, the percentage is 72.8%. States with limited branching rights in which MBHCs control less than half the deposits have a concentration percentage of 70.1%. Unit banking states in which MBHCs control more than half the deposits have a concentration percentage of 71.9%. The only exception is for unit banking states in which MBHCs control less than half the deposits. For these states, the concentration percentage is 56%.[112] Thus, the degree to which banks could expand intrastate has had little or no effect on the average concentration of banking resources locally despite the pronounced tendency of less restrictive policies to encourage concentration on a statewide basis. Accordingly, it can be inferred that no change in concentration would occur after the enactment of interstate banking and thrift legislation even if regional and national concentration levels increase.

B. The Effect on Deposit Flows.

A persistent theme of opponents of interstate legislation has been the argument that out-of-state institutions will enter a given market for the purpose of siphoning off deposits and redeploying these funds in other geographic markets thereby causing a scarcity of money. Conversely, proponents of interstate banking have argued that the entry of new banks into a given market will mean increased funds available for lending for the area. Both arguments are open to question. The flow of deposit funds are controlled by market forces and absent some effective artificial constraint[113] on the operation of these forces, money will flow to where the demand for it exists.

Ironically, one study has persuasively demonstrated that it is small community banks rather than large regional or money center banks which generally act as conduits for a net outflow of deposits.[114] Large banks tend to deploy an average of only 28.5% of their total assets locally. However, they also derive only 26.2% of their funds locally. Thus, the ratio of local uses to local sources is 1.1. Large banks then are net importers of funds to local markets. This is primarily because large banks depend not on local deposits for their funds but rather on the interbank and other financial markets. Thus, although they respond to lending opportunities on a national basis, they also fund these loans through the national markets.

---
112. Rhoades, *supra* Note 98. At the time this data was compiled, only three states had unit banking laws in which MBHCs controlled less than half the deposits.
113. Artificial constraints do exist. Kentucky, New Jersey, Ohio and West Virginia all prohibit acquisitions which increase deposit concentration levels above certain limits and Pennsylvania and Maryland require institutions to offer basic transaction account services. In general, however, these restrictions are not effective because of the ability of financial institutions to solicit deposits by mail.
114. *See, generally,* C. Dunham, Interstate Banking and the Outflow of Local Funds, New England Economic Review March/April 1986 (hereinafter Dunham) for a discussion of deposit flows and the statistics contained in this section.

By contrast, small banks tend to make almost all their loans locally but actually deploy only an average of 56.8% of their assets locally. At the same time, they derive 95.4% of their funds locally. As a consequence, small banks have a ratio of local uses to local sources of .6 and are therefore net exporters of funds. There are several reasons for this. Small banks do not have the same ready access to the interbank and other financial markets that large banks do and therefore are forced to rely on nonloan assets such as government securities and federal funds for liquidity. More fundamentally, the customers of small banks are individuals who generally are net suppliers of funds. Also, small banks do not have the same loan demand as large banks. Therefore, they often have excess funds that they deploy nonlocally.

The foregoing discussion refutes the suggestion that the breakdown of geographic barriers will significantly alter the flow of funds. The fact that local banks are already net exporters of funds and large banks net importers reveals that the banking system already acts as a geographic intermediary for the flow of funds, regardless of the existence of interstate barriers. Excess demand for funds in one region is reflected in increased rates offered in the interbank and other financial markets and local banks investing in these nonloan assets are indirect lenders to the region in which the excess demand originated.[115]

Another question concerning the effect of interstate legislation on the flow of funds is to what extent does the affiliation of smaller banks with large bank holding companies alter the flow of funds? Empirical evidence suggests that, in general, small banks affiliated with larger parent organizations do behave differently than independent banks of the same size.[116] In general, affiliated banks begin to offer more sophisticated services, and to the extent a demand for these services exists, the result can be a net inflow of funds. The likely customers for such services are larger businesses that previously sought banking services elsewhere. Conversely, there also is a new nonlocal outlet for funds through the parent organization. This could result in a net outflow of funds. However, the first source of funds for this new nonlocal outlet is generally the nonloan liquid assets in which small banks invest their excess funds such as government securities. Accordingly, rather than cause a net outflow of funds, affiliation generally causes only a redirection of the ultimate use of exported funds from nonlocal, nonloan assets to nonlocal lending opportunities.

Thus, the extent to which affiliation with a large bank holding company by a small bank may cause a net outflow of funds from the small bank will depend on the strength of the local demand for the new services that the local banks can offer versus the opportunity for nonlocal investment. In short, the same market forces which have always driven deposit flows will continue to do so. If local demand exists, funds will be retained locally to meet the demand; if demand does not exist, funds will be exported.

---

115. Dunham, *supra* Note 114, p. 10.
116. Dunham, *supra* Note 100, page 15.

C. The Regional Market Focus.

One of the most important effects of the legislation and ensuing consolidation will be the shift in geographic market focus of the industry. Until recently the geographic market focus of large commercial banks has been confined to Pennsylvania because legislation precluded any other possibilities. Even the statewide focus of the larger banks is a relatively recent phenomenon which did not begin in earnest until legislation authorizing limited statewide expansion was enacted in 1982. Smaller banks generally have a narrow market view. With respect to thrifts, this parochial focus is even more pronounced. Only three Pennsylvania thrifts have any significant statewide presence.[117] Many thrifts not only have a very local outlook but actually can trace their origins to a particular ethnic group or church.

In the past two years the larger banks have begun to adjust their focus to the regional level in anticipation of the enactment of interstate legislation and the prospects for regional expansion. Smaller banks, while not generally focusing on regional expansion, have, or are beginning, to at least recognize the increased competitive threat that regional banking entails and the opportunities it presents.

The shift from a parochial to a regional focus will be the most dramatic for thrifts although it probably will not occur as readily as in the banking industry. The larger thrifts have begun to prepare for regional and perhaps national competition and expansion, but the smaller thrifts, especially those located in urban areas, must recognize and plan for increased competitive pressures from new entrants to the market. Initially, this increased competition will probably come from new banks entering the market and therefore the competition will focus on attracting deposits since thrifts and banks generally serve different loan markets. However, as thrifts begin to expand their product line, increased competition should span the spectrum of products and services.

Another factor which makes the likelihood of regional consolidation such a dramatic change for thrifts is that significant intrastate consolidation has not even occurred among Pennsylvania thrifts. Since 1982, intrastate consolidation has proceeded in the banking industry and therefore the coming interstate consolidation can be seen as a logical progression. Thrifts, on the other hand, will experience both intrastate and interstate consolidation simultaneously.[118] The primary reason that intrastate consolidation among thrifts has not occurred is that the large majority of Pennsylvania thrifts are mutual institutions. Although mergers between mutual institutions can and do occur, such transactions have not occurred at a pace sufficient

---

117. Atlantic Financial, F.A., Hill Financial Savings Association and Horizon Financial, F.A. have a presence in more than one geographic market in the state. Both Atlantic Financial and Meritor Financial Group, however, have expanded interstate.

118. This may present certain economic advantages to thrifts because expansion will proceed based upon market considerations unconstrained by artificial geographic boundaries. This opportunity to expand into natural markets could generate certain economies of scale and allow thrifts to take advantage of growth opportunities that were not available to commercial banks. For example, in 1982, the large Philadelphia banks surely would have chosen Southern New Jersey as a growth market and expanded there had they been permitted to do so. Notwithstanding the advantages that regional consolidation versus intrastate consolidation will provide, the coming transformation of the thrift industry will be as, if not more significant, than the interest rate shocks of the 1970s.

to generate the competitive pressures which forced intrastate consolidation in the banking industry. The conversion of mutual thrifts to stock thrifts is accelerating, however. At December 31, 1986, 20 Pennsylvania thrifts have converted. This is approximately twice the number of stock thrifts which existed at the end of 1985. Many others will be considering conversion because the FSLIC recently increased the capital requirements imposed on thrifts from a minimum of 3% to a minimum of 6%. This requirement will be phased in over a period estimated to be from 6 to 12 years depending on industry profitability and the easiest way to meet the new rules will be through conversion or a merger conversion with an existing stock thrift. The expansion of stock institutions, together with the new capital rules,[119] may generate competitive pressures which will force other mutuals to convert and consolidate. In addition, the pace of thrift conversions and thrift consolidations will be affected by changes in interest rates and the accompanying affect on thrift earnings, the health of the FSLIC insurance fund and the traditional independence of thrift managers.

In the final analysis, the management of banks and thrifts must recognize that the rules are new and both the playing field and the roster of players has grown dramatically. Those managers that do recognize these facts and plan accordingly should be the most successful.

D. The Regional Landscape.[120]

Consolidation for both banks and thrifts seems inevitable. If that is the case, what will the financial industry in Pennsylvania look like in the coming years? What criteria will determine what goals are available and what strategies should be employed to reach these goals?

The logical outcome of regional[121] consolidation in the banking industry is the market dominance of a few large bank holding companies. Prior to 1990, the regional banking market probably will be dominated, both in terms of deposit concentration and significant lending markets, by eight to ten bank holding companies with assets in excess of $8 to $10 billion.[122] Of these, at least four or five will be Pennsylvania-based bank holding companies. As full interstate banking approaches, however, consolidation will increase significantly the asset size which will be needed to retain a dominant share of the market and institutional independence. In the long run, the region is likely to be dominated by about five super regionals with assets in excess of $20 billion.

---

119. 12 C.F.R. §563.13.

120. An important resource material utilized in the preparation of this section was a report prepared by McKinsey and Company, Inc. for the Bank Administration Institute entitled "Banker's Merger and Acquisition Choices — Mapping a Course through Consolidation." Hereinafter, the "McKinsey Report."

121. For purposes of this discussion the region includes the states named in Pennsylvania's bank and thrift bills except Virginia and the District of Columbia which are excluded because Pennsylvania bank holding companies and thrifts cannot enter either jurisdiction.

122. At present, only eight banks in the seven state region have assets in excess of $10 billion. These institutions are likely to remain independent for the short term and may be joined by one or two others.

Merger activity should be greatest among bank holding companies with assets of between $1 and $8 billion with two goals in mind. Entities may merge in an attempt to be one of the long term surviving super regionals or they may consolidate with a view to selling at a later date. They, of course, can also maintain their independence and grow internally.

Because intrastate consolidation has not occurred to the same extent in the thrift industry as in the banking industry, it is impossible to make predictions concerning regional dominance. This is especially true because of the approximately thirty-five institutions in the region with over $1 billion in assets as of March 31, 1986, only thirteen are stock institutions. Moreover, of the approximately thirteen institutions in the region with assets in excess of $2 billion, only eight are stock thrifts.[123] It seems probable that stock thrifts rather than mutuals are most likely to expand through mergers and acquisitions for a number of reasons. Any merger between mutual thrifts must be strictly by mutual consent. A stock thrift can also form a holding company and thus offer an acquiree an opportunity to operate as an independent subsidiary of the holding company. Finally, stock thrifts have a greater access to capital and therefore may be more able to fund the cost of acquisitions.[124] Accordingly, it is entirely possible that a stock thrift with assets of less than $1 billion could begin an acquisition campaign of mutual institutions through the use of the merger conversion process[125] and become one of the dominant thrifts in its state if not the region.

Although both the banking and thrift industries may come to be dominated by super regionals, that does not mean that all remaining financial institutions will fade into oblivion. In both the banking and thrift industries, small and medium size community institutions will survive in significant numbers. This will be especially true in rural parts of the region because many rural areas will not be perceived as attractive markets by the larger financial institutions. This is not to say that community banks will go unchanged. It is likely that they too will begin to associate with each other through franchising operations or confederation arrangements. They may also serve as marketing outlets for the products of larger institutions. Finally, they may join bank or thrift holding company structures that are essentially associations of independent banks or thrifts that share certain functions at the holding company level such as data processing in order to increase productivity and decrease marginal costs.

Two other types of institutions which may survive and flourish are low-cost, efficient banks and thrifts and those that serve a particular market niche. Obviously, these types are not mutually exclusive nor are they necessarily incompatible with smaller community banks. Small efficient banks may very well prosper in the future by offering attractive deposit and lending rates made possible by low overhead.

---

123. Based on FHLBB published statistics as of March 31, 1986.
124. Even though no consideration passes between the parties to a merger of mutual institutions, the process can still be costly and time consuming.
125. It is important to note that merger conversions do not require an expenditure of capital but actually increases the capital of the resulting entity. Thus, it is quite conceivable that an institution ranging in size between $500 million to $1 billion could grow rapidly through merger conversions.

Many of these competitors will be *de novo* entrants into the financial services industry. This trend has already commenced in Pennsylvania. For example, despite the intrastate consolidation of recent years, the number of banking institutions in both Philadelphia and Allegheny Counties has actually increased from 1976 to 1985.[126] In particular, *de novo* entries to the Philadelphia SMSA have experienced success.

"Boutique" institutions that focus upon a particular market should also enjoy some success. For certain larger institutions this may mean focusing on particular sophisticated lending transactions or particular business customers. The obvious example of these types of banks are some of the larger New York banks such as Bankers Trust or Morgan Guaranty who forego consumer banking in favor of corporate and international banking. On a smaller scale, many bank and thrift institutions may flourish by concentrating on, and providing personalized services to, a particular individual customer segment such as urban professionals.

E. Criteria for Determining Strategy.[127]

The most important function management of a bank or thrift can perform in connection with the coming consolidation is to accurately and honestly assess the strengths and weaknesses of their institution, and, based on this assessment, choose an attainable goal and plan accordingly. The manager should carefully evaluate a number of factors concerning the institution including: (1) capital adequacy; (2) asset size; (3) market capitalization; (4) managerial depth; and (5) franchise area.

From a regulatory perspective, capital adequacy of an institution is an important determinant of an institution's ability to embark on any acquisition campaign and to compete vigorously. Both banking and thrift regulators have recently increased their emphasis on the capital ratio of an institution resulting from a merger or acquisition. As a result, in more and more cash transactions, the target's equity is replaced either by the acquiror's equity or other capital securities to maintain a strong capital position. However, to the extent an acquiror uses debt not qualifying as capital to fund an acquisition, the capital of the acquiror alone must be sufficient to allow the resulting institution to meet its capital requirements.

Clearly, the asset size of an institution will have a bearing upon the goals which its management chooses. It would be unrealistic for most firms to entertain any notion that they will play a significant regional role simply because this would require significant growth. The super regionals in banking will come from the ranks of the largest existing firms or the combination of two or more firms of relatively equal size into a new giant.[128]

Perhaps of even more importance than absolute size, however, is the market capitalization of a bank or thrift. This is true because the "currency" of merger and

---

126. Pennsylvania Bank Stock Annual 1985, Ryan, Beck & Co.
127. *See* generally the McKinsey Report, *supra* Note 120 for further discussion of the issues discussed in this section.
128. As noted, this requirement of large asset size is not as applicable for thrifts. Clearly, however, a $100 million thrift cannot reasonably seek a large regional role.

acquisition transactions is usually the stock of the acquiror. Stock of the acquiror is often issued to the shareholders of the target in a tax-free exchange. Alternatively, stock may be issued to the public to raise funds for a cash transaction. Accordingly, the market value of an institution's stock determines how much of its "currency" it must expend to make a given acquisition. An institution whose stock is valued more highly than the stock of another institution can issue less stock than the other institution in order to effect the same acquisition and thereby reduce the "cost" of the acquisition, in terms of dilution, to the acquiror's shareholders. The stockholders of the entity whose stock is valued less highly will experience more dilution and the stock price and total market capitalization of the institution may fall.[129] This may result in an inability to do a second or third acquisition or it may make the acquiror a target.

The cost of an acquisition is also a function of the total market capitalization of the acquiree. Although book value rather than market capitalization is often the valuation standard utilized in reporting merger and acquisition transactions, it would be the rare transaction indeed in which the acquiror pays *less* than the market capitalization of the target because the target's Board of Directors would be hard-pressed to accept such a price. Accordingly, the market capitalization of an acquiree generally can be viewed as a floor on any acquisition price. Accordingly, it is market capitalization, *not asset size,* which should determine who can acquire whom. Market capitalization is related to profitability. For example, some of the highly successful regional banks have extraordinarily high total market capitalizations because of their excellent earnings performance. Moreover, the performance of the money center banks has not kept pace with the super regionals in recent years, and this is reflected in their relative stock prices. The absolute cost to acquire these super regionals would be quite high and accordingly only a few money center banks may attempt such an acquisition because it could entail unacceptable dilution. Thus, managers should analyze the market capitalization of their institution in relation to the market capitalization of its regional competitors to determine which entities are potential acquirors of the institution and which may be attractive acquisition candidates. Moreover, they should strive for excellent earnings performance in order to keep market capitalization high from both an offensive and defensive perspective.

The importance of skilled management is another element which managers must evaluate. The integration of an acquired institution into the existing structure of an acquiror is a time consuming and demanding task that requires depth of management. Yet the task is crucial if an acquiror expects to justify a premium acquisition by improving performance of the acquiree. An institution whose management is already stretched thin in the conduct of its own operation must be wary of taking on the task of improving the performance of another entity.

Another factor which must be evaluated by the management of a bank or thrift is its franchise area from both a local and a regional perspective. Of importance is the growth potential of the market, demographic and economic trends in the market, the degree of competition in the local market and the position of the state in the

---

129. Unless the acquiring institution is itself viewed as a target in which case acceptable dilution levels may be higher.

region. An institution located in an area offering limited growth opportunities may seek growth through acquisitions in different geographic markets and the same factors which are important in evaluating an institution's home market are important in evaluating which new markets to enter.

Conversely, an institution which is located in an attractive market may be an acquisition candidate because of this fact. An institution in the latter situation that is not adverse to selling can seek out a number of bidders and in effect hold an auction. Other institutions in attractive markets who wish to remain independent should carefully evaluate their need for additional antitakeover protection. They may also seek to expand within their market through acquisitions to the extent they are permitted to do so by the antitrust laws and with due regard to the dilutive affect of any acquisition on market capitalization.

From a regional perspective, Pennsylvania is centrally located and there are a number of large and aggressive financial institutions based in Pennsylvania. Of the approximately eight bank holding companies in the region with assets in excess of $10 billion, four are located in Pennsylvania. It is these institutions that may be most inclined to seek regional prominence through acquisitions. Accordingly, in the banking industry, Pennsylvania institutions will likely be net acquirors.

With respect to specific institutions, those most likely to command attractive premimums are those located near state borders. This is because an acquiror who is just across the border from the target will be more able to effect cost reductions and realize other economies of scale with respect to the target as opposed to an institution that is more distant. Therefore, the acquiror can expect to earn out any dilution more quickly and accordingly afford a higher premium.

With respect to thrifts, again, the answer is less clear. Ohio and New Jersey both have more large thrifts over $1 billion in assets than does Pennsylvania and more of these are stock institutions.[130] Perhaps more importantly, Ohio has many more stock thrifts than either Pennsylvania or New Jersey. At December 31, 1986, approximately 60 Ohio thrifts were stock thrifts while Pennsylvania had only 20 stock thrifts and New Jersey had only 8 stock thrifts.[131] Thus, at present, Ohio thrifts seem to be the most capable of expanding interstate. However, conversions in Pennsylvania are currently proceeding at a brisk pace and are likely to continue if interest rates remain low and the market for thrift stocks does not decline. These newly converted institutions will likely harbor some acquisition-minded management personnel and therefore predictions concerning which state in the region is likely to be a net acquiror in the thrift industry is premature.

---

130. Ohio has 14 thrifts with assets of more than $1 billion and six of these institutions are stock thrifts. New Jersey has nine such institutions and three are stock thrifts. Pennsylvania has eight institutions with assets of over $1 billion, but only two are stock thrifts. Based on FHLBB published statistics as of March 31, 1986.
131. Based on information supplied by Ryan, Beck & Co.

F. Goals and Strategies.

Once management has carefully evaluated the relative position of the institution, an attainable goal or goals must be chosen and a strategy designed to accomplish these goal or goals. Each goal has its risks and management must be aware of these. The most effective plan is one that has two goals, a primary and secondary goal, and a flexible strategy that permits the institution to switch from the first to the second goal.[132] For buyers, this generally means recognizing when further expansion is unwarranted and knowing when and if to sell. For long-term sellers, this may mean recognizing the right offer when it is presented even if it is before the institution intended to sell. Discussed below are some of the options available for different types of institutions.

Large Bank Holding Companies. Bank holding companies with assets of about $8 to $10 billion are the firms that can reach for regional prominence. As previously discussed, the optimum size required to play a future leading role in the region will probably be over $20 billion.[133] This means that a sequence of acquisitions or perhaps a marriage of equals will be necessary. In order to achieve these goals, the institution must have a high market capitalization and management depth.

Major risks accompany this strategy. The acquiror may not be able to integrate acquisitions effectively and therefore fail to earn out any dilution. As a result, profitability and stock price will suffer with a resulting adverse impact on the ability to make subsequent acquisitions. Also, an institution's capital could decrease materially and therefore hamper growth through acquisitions. As a result, the institution will fail to achieve its goal of regional dominance and performance may suffer as well. The danger of falling short of the goal is that the institution may be too large for another institution to acquire easily. Premiums for large institutions are generally less than those for smaller ones. The market will recognize both the failure to achieve the desired goal and the lack of attraction the institution has as an acquisition candidate and therefore the stock price will fall. This, of course, further hampers growth.

Medium Size Bank Holding Companies. Bank holding companies between $1 and $8 billion in assets have a number of choices. The larger institutions among this group may still seek to become one of the super regionals. This could entail a marriage of equals in which little or no premium is paid, or a series of good size acquisitions.

The dangers of a strategy designed to maximize growth through acquisitions, which were highlighted above for large bank holding companies, are also present here but are magnified simply because greater growth is required. In addition, a strategy that begins with a marriage of equals faces the additional problem of integrating two large organizations. This often takes more time and may produce fewer benefits because of an inability to cut costs quickly.

---

132. *See* generally, the McKinsey Report *supra* Note 120 for further discussion of the issues addressed in this section.
133. The McKinsey Report suggests that the required asset size may be even greater in the long term and may actually be closer to $40 to $50 billion.

Another choice for these institutions is to make a series of wise acquisitions and then sell, possibly in 1990 when full interstate banking arrives. The purpose of the acquisition would be to assemble a holding company with banking subsidiaries which are either superior performers or in attractive markets, or both, with a view to attracting multiple bidders. If inter-industry barriers between the banking and thrift industry continue to erode, this may include the acquisition of stock thrifts or mutual thrifts in merger conversion transactions. The key to this strategy will be to effectively integrate the acquisitions in order to create value. Failure to do so could result in a relatively large, low performing holding company which is unable to sell at an acceptable premium, although to the extent the resulting institution has a presence in attractive markets, it will retain value. This strategy must also be weighed against the risk that acquisition premiums could fall. An argument can be made that acquisition premiums presently appear high only because the stock price of most acquirors is at historically high levels. If stock prices declined, acquisition premiums may do so as well. Moreover, if stock prices declined, market capitalization will fall and these institutions may become susceptible to nonnegotiated tender or exchange offers because they are more affordable.

The other choices for these institutions is to maintain independence and concentrate on improving performance or consider joining a confederation or franchising arrangement. Improved performance, of course, has its own rewards, but it can also help an institution to sell at a high premium if this is desired later. If an eventual sale is desired, then implicit in this strategy is the belief that buyers will appear after the improvement occurs and full interstate banking becomes a reality. The danger, of course, is that buyers do not emerge or that performance does not improve. A stakeout agreement in which an institution agrees to be acquired at a future date and at a price dependent on performance may be another alternative. This may permit an institution to lock in a certain premium yet still permit further gains in price if performance improves.

Small Banks and Bank Holding Companies. Smaller banks and bank holding companies with assets of less than $1 billion also have a number of options depending upon their condition. Small, weak banks should consider taking aggressive steps to correct deficiencies in order to remain independent. This may involve new structures such as a franchising arrangement. Alternatively, such institutions may consider selling now, with due regard to the market for bank stocks generally, while interstate banking is new and new entrants to the market appear and while larger banks seek to grow in size in order to become regional players or to position themselves as a target. The danger in selling now is that if performance is likely to improve, the institution may forego a higher price. The alternative may be to seek improvement and wait for full interstate banking and the second wave of acquirors from New York and other states. The risk of waiting is that the size of attractive acquisition candidates may increase dramatically and smaller institutions will be passed over or, alternatively stock prices and acquisition premiums may fall. Again, if stock prices fall, small institutions become more vulnerable to nonnegotiated tender or exchange offers.

Small, strong performers could also sell now but they clearly run the danger of foregoing a higher price later if more suitors enter the market in 1990. Four alternatives exist. They could seek further improvement in performance and hopefully command an exceptional premium when other bidders arrive. They could also enter into stakeout agreements now in which they agree to be acquired at a future date and at a price which is dependent upon their performance. This agreement might contain a minimum price which would protect stockholders in the event performance declines yet give them the opportunity to share in any gains realized as a result of improved performance. Another alternative would be to seek a limited number of wise acquisitions with the goal of reaching the size of the most attractive future acquisition candidates. If inter-industry barriers erode, this may include the acquisition of stock thrifts or mutual thrifts in merger conversion transactions. The risk of this strategy is the failure to earn out dilution and enhance value thereby making a small, strong performer a medium-sized, weak institution.

The final choice for these institutions is to maintain independence. In order to do this, an institution should make an effort to improve the liquidity of the market for its stock in order to keep the relative price high. This can be accomplished by a second offering to increase the number of shares in the market. Institutions in rural areas will be most able to retain independence because larger bank holding companies may not view the rural market as a particularly attractive one.

Thrifts. Thrifts come in two forms, mutual and stock. Both types of thrifts can and do merge and are likely to continue to do so on an interstate basis.[134] On balance, however, it seems more likely that stock thrifts will lead the way in merger activity because they can form holding companies more readily, raise capital to fund acquisitions and meet the FHLBB's new capital requirements.[135]

Accordingly, until more thrifts convert, a significant increase in merger activity is not likely. Even when larger numbers of thrifts have converted to stock ownership, however, there may be a lull before merger and acquisition activity increases significantly. Many of the thrifts that convert may do so because of regulatory capital concerns. As a result, they may feel the need to accumulate capital before they implement any acquisition strategy. A number of second thrift stock offerings are likely if the market remains receptive and interest rates remain low.

A second deterrent to rapid merger and acquisition activity in the thrift industry will be that the newly converted thrifts may choose to form holding companies before embarking on acquisition campaigns. The process of converting to stock ownership and then forming a holding company in general will take about one to two years.[136] Therefore, even with the spate of recent Pennsylvania thrift conversions, it is unlikely that merger and acquisition activity will begin to accelerate until the

---

134. In fact, some very large mutual thrift institutions have arisen as a result of mergers.
135. Under the FHLBB's capital rules a merger must result in an institution that complies with the FHLBB's capital rules. Because mutuals cannot raise capital by issuing new stock, mergers between mutuals would have to be between institutions that together meet the capital rules. Since many thrifts currently do not meet these new rules, many potential transactions may be precluded. In addition, executives of mutual institutions have historically demonstrated a desire to maintain independence and therefore a reluctance to merge.
136. A conversion directly from mutual form to a holding company structure is possible and is occurring with increasing frequency.

latter part of 1987, if then. Discussed below are possible scenarios for different size thrifts.

Large Stock Thrifts. Stock thrifts with assets of over $500 million can reasonably attempt to implement an acquisition strategy designed to achieve regional prominence. Normally, the size disparity between institutions of $500 million and the largest Pennsylvania thrift, Meritor Financial Group with assets of almost $13 billion,[137] would be too great for these smaller thrifts to seriously entertain an attempt to compete for regional superiority. However, two factors may permit such a scenario. First, significant consolidation has not yet occurred in Pennsylvania. There are over one hundred thrifts in Pennsylvania with assets of between $100 million and $500 million. One acquisition of a large thrift in this category or two acquisitions of smaller thrifts in this category could easily place thrifts with assets of between $500 million to $1 billion in a competitive regional position.

Perhaps more importantly, to the extent thrift acquisitions are accomplished through merger conversions, capital is increased rather than expended.[138] Moreover, the price an acquiror pays for a thrift in a merger conversion is determined by independent appraisal. Recently appraisal values for conversions have been between 50% and 65% of the pro forma book value of the thrift after conversion. Subsequent to conversion and over time, the market has valued thrifts at approximately book value or slightly less and frequently prices of recently converted thrift stocks have risen. Presumably this reflects some assessment of earnings strength. To the extent that purchasers in merger conversions buy at less than the pro forma book value, merger conversions are unlikely to cause unacceptable dilution.

Of course, merger conversions are not the only transactions likely to take place. Mergers and acquisitions between stock thrifts will probably occur. The analysis of which institutions can achieve a significant regional position as a result of transactions between stock thrifts parallels the analysis for bank holding companies. Thrifts with assets in excess of $1 billion will stand the best chance of establishing a large regional role. Medium-sized thrifts with assets between $500 million and $1 billion will have a chance to do so but to the extent they must do so through the acquisition of stock thrifts and the concomitant expenditure of capital and/or dilution, their chances will be diminished. Keys to success for all these thrifts will be the same as for banks. A high market capitalization (in comparison to other thrifts) and the managerial ability to integrate the target into the organization.[139]

Small Stock Thrifts. Small stock thrifts of less than $500 million enjoy a wide range of options because consolidation has not yet occurred and not many stock institutions exist. The first option may be to sell. Because few small stock thrifts exist and merger conversion candidates may be difficult to find for the larger acquisition-minded thrifts, the small stock thrifts could be attractive acquisition

---

137. It is important to note that Meritor is by far the largest thrift in the state. The next largest, Atlantic Financial, had assets of $4.8 billion as of September 30, 1986.
138. Of course, the acquiror is then faced with the problem of deploying this capital and earning a satisfactory return in order to maintain its stock price.
139. In general, thrift stocks trade at or slightly below book value. Therefore, market capitalization in relation to other thrifts rather than in comparison to banks will be important.

candidates and command a high premium. The risk in this strategy is that the effect of the FHLBB's new interstate branching regulation, especially the supervisory portion of that regulation which will permit entry of thrifts from outside the region, is not yet known. It may greatly increase the universe of bidders, thus increasing prices. An institution that sells now may be sold cheaply in comparison to future prices. Conversely, if the number of bidders is not increased as a result of the FHLBB regulation, the absence of a national trigger in Pennsylvania's interstate thrift legislation would militate in favor of a sale to a regional bidder.

Other alternatives for these stock thrifts will be to maintain independence or make their own acquisitions, either through merger conversions or through the acquisition of stock thrifts. This could be done with a view to future sale.

Mutual Thrifts. Mutual thrifts can merge with other thrifts in consensual transactions. The difficulty will be in finding willing partners with capital levels such that, upon completion of the merger, the resulting institution will comply with regulatory requirements. Another impediment to mergers between mutuals is that the parties do not owe a fiduciary duty to shareholders and therefore are under little or no pressure to accept any offer. Mutual mergers, perhaps more than other transactions, require the accommodation of management egos first and foremost.

Alternatively, a mutual thrift can convert to stock ownership and then expand. The question will be whether to convert directly or enter into a merger conversion. It is important to note that a merger conversion does not necessitate a loss of control. A large mutual thrift could enter into a merger conversion with a smaller stock thrift with the management of the former controlling the resulting institution. In general, the best course appears to be to convert first and then seek merger partners. This is because the price in a merger conversion is determined by an independent appraisal rather than negotiation. As noted, appraisal values have recently been between 50% and 65% of the pro forma book value of the converted institution. After conversion, post-conversion stock prices have generally appreciated. Thus, in a merger conversion in which the acquiror will be the surviving institution, management of the target will have sold the institution at a discount rather than a premium. Moreover, in the transaction, stock of the acquiror is offered for sale to depositors, management and employees of the target and the public and the proceeds are used to purchase newly issued stock of the target. This new capital goes into the institution, not to depositors and management. If an institution first converts and then sells at a negotiated premium, all those who have invested in the target in the initial conversion will realize the premium.

In the case of a merger conversion in which the management of a mutual institution is supposed to control the resulting entity, a different problem arises. The price for the transaction will be set by the appraisal but the actual amount of stock which the acquiror offers will be a function of its market price. Therefore, the amount of stock which the depositors, management and employees of the mutual thrift can actually acquire will fluctuate during the pendency of the transaction. If the stock price of the acquiror increases, the percentage ownership of the resulting institution that the depositors, management and employees of the mutual thrift will acquire will decrease. A transaction that was designed to give control to the management of the mutual thrift could actually result in something quite different.

It might be expected that if acquisitions of stock thrifts occur at book value or a premium to book value, appraisal values in conversions or merger conversions will rise. This may, in fact, occur, but until such time, it appears that a standard conversion is preferable to a merger conversion for the depositors and management of mutual thrifts.

VII. CONCLUSION

As a result of the passage of interstate bank and thrift legislation and the adoption by the FHLBB of new interstate branching regulations, the composition of the financial services industry in Pennsylvania will change dramatically. The number of banks and thrifts will most likely decline markedly over an extended period of time but the strength of the remaining institutions should be enhanced. Large super regional banks and thrifts who survive will dominate the region in both deposit and loan volume. Nevertheless, smaller community banks and thrifts may well survive and flourish in the new environment because they will offer personalized service to consumers and, perhaps better prices on smaller loans. Acquisition activity should accelerate as a result of the new legislation if market conditions are favorable and financial institution executives can expect to lead busy, stimulating lives.

EXHIBIT "A"
THE GENERAL ASSEMBLY OF PENNSYLVANIA
SENATE BILL
No. 1075 — Session of 1985
AN ACT

Amending the act of November 30, 1965 (P.L. 847, No. 356), entitled "An act relating to and regulating the business of banking and the exercise by corporations of fiduciary powers; affecting persons engaged in the business of banking and corporations exercising fiduciary powers and affiliates of such persons; affecting the shareholders of such persons and the directors, trustees, officers, attorneys and employees of such persons and of the affiliates of such persons; affecting national banks located in the Commonwealth; affecting persons dealing with persons engaged in the business of banking, corporations exercising fiduciary powers and national banks; conferring powers and imposing duties on the Banking Board, on certain departments and officers of the Commonwealth and on courts, prothonotaries, clerks and recorders of deeds; providing penalties; and repealing certain acts and parts of acts," authorizing acquisitions of bank holding companies and banks in Pennsylvania by bank holding companies located in other states on a regional, reciprocal basis for a certain period of time and on a reciprocal basis without a regional requirement thereafter.

The General Assembly makes the following findings as the basis for this act:

(1) The rapid development of interstate banking in recent years can be expected to continue and to have significant effects on the business of commercial banking in the Commonwealth by reasons of the economic, regulatory, financial and technological forces that affect the business.

(2) It is in the best interests of the economy of this Commonwealth and its public to enable commercial banks in this Commonwealth to remain sound, strong and competitive with banks located elsewhere and with other financial organizations.

(3) As an increasing number of other states authorize interstate banking in some form, banks and bank holding companies in this Commonwealth would be disadvantaged if not permitted to combine with banks and bank holding companies elsewhere.

(4) A fundamental change in the banking structure to accommodate interstate banking can be made in a more orderly manner and with an opportunity for participation by banks of all sizes by an authorization of interstate combinations in a limited regional area during an initial period of time before reciprocal banking without a regional requirement is permitted.

The General Assembly of the Commonwealth of Pennsylvania hereby enacts as follows:

Section 1. Section 115(b)(i) of the act of November 10, 1965 (P.L. 847, No. 356), known as the Banking Code of 1965, added March 4, 1982 (P.L. 135, No. 44), is amended to read:

Section 115. Bank Holding Companies

***

(b) Control of institutions —

(i) No bank holding company other than a Pennsylvania bank holding company may control an institution except as expressly provided in Section 116 with respect to bank holding companies in other states.

***

Section 2. The act is amended by adding a section to read:

Section 116. Authorization of Reciprocal Interstate Banking

(a) Definitions — As used in this section:

(i) "Bank," "bank holding company" and "control" — shall have the same meanings as those terms have under the Federal Bank Holding Company Act (60 Stat. 133, Public Law 84-511) and regulations of the Federal Reserve Board as in effect from time to time and the terms "acquire" and "acquisition" shall include any transaction under such act and regulations. A bank holding company shall be deemed to be "located" in the state in which the total deposits of all its bank subsidiaries are largest.

(ii) "Institutions" and "Pennsylvania Bank Holding Company" — shall have the same meanings as those terms are defined in Section 115(a).

(iii) "Region" — shall mean, in addition to this state, the states of Delaware, Kentucky, Maryland, New Jersey, Ohio, Virginia, West Virginia and the District of Columbia.

(iv) "Domestic deposits" of a bank or a bank holding company — shall mean all deposits in offices in the United States, as determined by the most recent report of condition of such bank, or, in the case of such bank holding company, its bank subsidiaries, other than deposits in:

(A) A bank in which shares may be lawfully acquired without approval under the Federal Bank Holding Company Act.

(B) A bank acquired pursuant to Section 13(f) of the Federal Deposit Insurance Act (64 Stat. 873, Public Law 82-30).

(C) An international banking facility.

(v) "State" — shall also include the District of Columbia.

(b) Acquisitions by bank holding companies in other states — A bank holding company located in another state may acquire control of an institution or a Pennsylvania bank holding company or five percent or more of the voting shares of an institution or Pennsylvania bank holding company if:

(i) The law of the state where the acquiring bank holding company is located, and the law of the state where any bank holding company which controls such acquiring bank holding company is located, satisfies in each case the reciprocity requirement of subsection (c).

(ii) The acquiring bank holding company and any bank holding company which controls it is, in each case, located in the region except that the requirement of location in the region will not be applicable to an acquisition consummated after March 4, 1990.

(iii) Immediately prior to the acquisition and after giving effect thereto, seventy-five percent of the total domestic deposits of the acquiring bank holding company and any bank holding company which controls it are in banks located in states in the region if the requirement of location in the region is at the time applicable under clause (ii) and in any event are in banks located in states which satisfy the reciprocity requirement of subsection (c).

(iv) The number of institutions controlled by a bank holding company located in another state as a result of such acquisition would not exceed the number of institutions which a Pennsylvania bank holding company would be authorized to control at that time.

(v) The acquisition has been approved by the department.

(c) Reciprocity requirement — The law of another state is reciprocal with this section to the extent it expressly authorizes Pennsylvania bank holding companies to acquire banks or bank holding companies located in that state on terms and conditions substantially no more restrictive than those applicable to such an acquisition by a bank holding company located in that state. For the purpose of determining whether the law of another state does or does not satisfy this reciprocity requirement:

(i) The law of a state will not satisfy the reciprocity requirement if a bank in that state which a Pennsylvania bank holding company is authorized to acquire is subject to restrictions on competition with banks located in that state or restrictions on deposit or commercial loans not generally applicable to banks located in that state.

(ii) The law of a state will not fail to satisfy the reciprocity requirement solely by reason of the fact that a Pennsylvania bank holding company would be subject to limitations or restrictions on an acquisition of a bank or a bank holding company located in that state which would also be applicable to an acquisition by a bank holding company located in that state or which do not materially limit the ability of Pennsylvania bank holding companies to acquire banks or bank holding companies located in that state generally.

(iii) The law of a state which permits an acquisition of a bank only on the condition that such bank has been in operation for some specified period of time will not satisfy the reciprocity requirement with respect to the acquisition of an institution which has not been in operation for at least the same period of time, except that this provision shall not prohibit the organization of a new institution solely to effect an acquisition otherwise permitted by this section.

(iv) The reciprocal interstate banking statute of each of the states of Kentucky, Maryland, Michigan, New Jersey, New York, Ohio, Rhode Island,

Utah, Washington and West Virginia shall be deemed reciprocal with this section in the form in which such statute existed on March 31, 1986. In the event of an amendment of any such statute, the determination whether it continues to be reciprocal with this section shall be made in accordance with this subsection in the same manner as the determination shall be made whether a statute of any state not specified in this clause is or is not reciprocal with this section.

(v) The department may determine whether the law of another state satisfies the reciprocity requirement.

(d) Approval by department — An application for approval by the department of an acquisition permitted by subsection (b) shall be made in such form and upon payment of such fee as the department shall prescribe and shall be supplemented by such additional information as the department shall request. Upon receipt of an application, the department shall conduct an investigation to determine whether to approve or disapprove the application on the basis of the financial and managerial resources of the applicant, the financial history and future prospects of the applicant and each institution and Pennsylvania bank holding company proposed to be acquired, any undue concentration of resources that would result from the acquisition and the convenience and needs of the public. In its investigation of the convenience and needs of the public, the department shall give specific attention to the effects of the acquisition on the availability, in this state, of those banking and basic transaction account services set forth in subsections (I) and (J). Within 60 days after receipt of the application or within such longer period not in excess of 30 days after receipt from the applicant of additional information requested by the department, the department shall approve or disapprove the proposed acquisition and give written notice of its decision to the applicant. In approving an acquisition under this section, the department may place conditions upon such approval and incorporate such terms and agreements as are deemed necessary to effect the purposes of this act.

(e) Change in circumstances — If a bank holding company located in another state which has acquired an institution or Pennsylvania bank holding company should have a change of circumstances so that at the time it would not satisfy the conditions of subsection (b) either by reason of a change in the place where it is located for the purpose of this section or by reason of the fact that it becomes subject to direct or indirect control by a bank holding company located in a state which does not satisfy the conditions of subsection (b), it shall divest control of each institution and Pennsylvania bank holding company which it controls prior to any voluntary combination which causes such change of circumstances or within one year (or such longer period of not more than an additional year as the department may permit in writing) after the occurrence of the reason other than a voluntary combination which caused the change of circumstances. A combination shall be deemed to be voluntary for the purpose of this subsection if an agreement or plan for such combination has been approved by a vote of the board of directors or a vote of the shareholders of the bank holding company located in another state which has acquired control of an institution or a Pennsylvania bank holding company.

(f) Effect of invalidity — The purpose of this section is solely to authorize reciprocal, regional banking for the initial period after the effective date of this section during which the requirement of location in the region is applicable under subsection (b) and reciprocal banking without a regional requirement thereafter to the extent expressly provided herein and this section shall not be construed to authorize any acquisition of control of an institution or Pennsylvania bank holding company by a bank holding company located in another state except as expressly provided in this section. In the event that any limitation on acquisitions of this section is held to be invalid by a final order of a court which is not subject to further review or appeal, or in the event that Section 3(d) of the Federal Bank Holding Company Act, or any substantially similar provision enacted in lieu thereof, is ruled by a final order of the United States Supreme Court either, within the period during which the requirement of location in the region is in effect under subsection (b), not to permit a regional restriction on interstate acquisitions of banks or bank holding companies or, at any time, not to permit a reciprocity requirement as a condition of such acquisition or, in either event, not to be valid to the extent it does so, the authorization of this section shall terminate immediately. Any acquisition consummated pursuant to this section prior to such termination shall not be affected thereby.

(g) Supervisory authority of department — The department shall have the same authority to require reports of condition from, and to examine, a bank holding company located in another state which acquires an institution or Pennsylvania bank holding company pursuant to this section as the authority it has to require reports of condition from, and to examine, Pennsylvania bank holding companies and to assess fees and collect expenses for such examinations. The department may accept examination reports in lieu of such examination and enter agreements with Federal and State banking regulators for exchange of information including examination reports.

(h) Acquisitions in other states by Pennsylvania bank holding companies — A Pennsylvania bank holding company which proposes to acquire a bank or bank holding company located in another state shall file an application for approval by the department in such form and upon payment of such fee as the department shall prescribe and shall supplement such application with such additional information as the department may reasonably request. The department shall conduct such investigation as it deems necessary to determine whether to approve or disapprove the application on the basis of the effects the proposed acquisition would have on the availability, in this state, of those banking services and basic transaction account services set forth in subsections (I) and (J). Within sixty days after receipt of the application or within such longer period, not in excess of thirty days, after receipt from the applicant of additional information requested by the department, the department shall approve or disapprove the proposed acquisition and give written notice of its decision to the applicant. In approving an acquisition under this section, the department may place conditions upon such approval and incorporate such terms and agreements as are deemed necessary to effect the purposes of this act.

(i) Availability of banking services — The department shall have the authority to assure that interstate banking acquisitions authorized by this section will not diminish reasonable availability of banking service to all segments of the public and economy of this state, with special emphasis on economic development and the financing of enterprises to the end that employment opportunities will be either increased or, where there is the prospect of reduction, retained. Upon receipt of an application for approval of an acquisition by a company located in another state under subsection (D) or approval of an acquisition in another state by a Pennsylvania bank holding company under subsection (B), the department shall review the credit practices and policies of each Pennsylvania bank holding company or institution which is involved in the proposed transaction. Such review shall determine the overall performance of such company or institution in providing credit and financial services to individuals and business enterprises in the communities which it serves in the light of its resources, its capital and its income, the particular needs of such communities, competition and alternative sources of credit. With respect to individuals, there shall be a review of consumer loans, residential mortgages, home improvement loans and student loans, particularly to residents of low-income and moderate-income neighborhoods. With respect to business enterprises, there shall be a review of extensions of credit and investments intended to promote economic development and creation, or retention where there is the prospect of reduction, of employment opportunities, including, without limitation, Small Business Administration and other small business loans, industrial development loans, financing of employee stock option plans and leveraged buy-outs of businesses by employees, financing of non-profit community development projects, loans and investments intended to maintain existing businesses and to encourage economic expansion and job opportunities, and loans and investments to promote participation by businesses in this state in international trade and to increase exports. The review by the department shall also include all other activities of the institution or company deemed to be suitable to its particular circumstances and the communities served. If the department determines that the overall performance of the institution or company has not been materially deficient and that it justifies the conclusion that the institution or company does and will provide suitable credit and financial services to its communities, it may approve the application without imposing any terms or conditions but otherwise may impose such terms and conditions as it deems appropriate to improve such overall performance over a stated period of time. The department shall, from time to time, review the continuing overall performance of each institution or company after an acquisition and, if it finds that its overall performance has not continued to be satisfactory, shall issue such order to the applicant as it deems appropriate.

(j) Availability of basic transaction account services — The department shall have the authority to assure that bank holding companies and institutions that become part of interstate banking organizations by reason of acquisition requiring approval under this section make basic transaction account services available to the public. For this purpose the department shall obtain, from all sources available to it or through such studies as it may commission, adequate information to determine:

(i) The needs of the public and, in particular, individuals with low or moderate income, for a basic checking or other transaction account.

(ii) The principal characteristics that such an account should have, such as the number of checks, deposits and other items for which a minimum charge may be made, the amount or rate of such minimum charge, and the forms of identification that may be required for opening and using such an account.

(iii) The existing availability of basic accounts with some or all of such principal characteristics currently offered by depository institutions, including applicants under this section, in separate communities of the state.

An applicant shall, at the request of the department, supply information to the department with respect to such accounts offered by each institution which is a subsidiary of applicant. The department may approve an application prior to the time it has acquired the information required by this section, but each institution which is a subsidiary of the applicant shall be subject, both before and after an approval of the acquisition under this section, to requirements imposed by the department, from time to time, to assure to the public, in the communities served by the institution, the continuing availability of the basic transaction account services which the department has determined the public needs.

(k) Establishment of advisory commission — For the purpose of advising the department in the conduct of its functions under subsections (i) and (j), there is hereby established an advisory commission, which shall consist of nine individuals selected as follows: five members appointed by the governor, one of whom may be selected from a list of at least three names submitted by the Pennsylvania Bankers Association, one of whom may be selected from a list of at least three names submitted by the Association of Savings Institutions, one of whom may be selected from a list of at least three names submitted by the Pennsylvania Credit Union League, one of whom shall have been selected by the governor to broadly represent business interests and one of whom shall have been selected by the governor to broadly represent consumer interest; one member each appointed by the president pro tempore and the minority leader of the Senate and the Speaker and minority leader of the House of Representatives. The term of the initial member of the Advisory Commission shall be until December 31, 1988 and the term of each member thereafter shall be two calendar years. The Secretary of Banking shall meet with the Advisory Commission at least quarterly for the first year, thereafter at least annually. Each member shall be entitled to receive travel and related expenses and such per diem honorarium as the department shall determine to be paid from the fees received by the department under this section. The Advisory Commission shall provide information, opinions and recommendations as to guidelines the department may establish, from time to time, for the purpose of determining the overall performance of an institution or company under subsection (i) and the availability of basic transaction account services under subsection (j). All decisions and determinations made under this section shall be made by the department.

(1) Enforcement — The department shall have the authority to issue regulations to carry out the provisions of this section and to issue orders to enforce the provisions of this section and its regulations thereunder, subject to the standards for exercise of power and discretion by the department under Section 103.

Section 3. All acts and parts of acts are repealed insofar as they are inconsistent with this act.

Section 4. This act shall take effect in 60 days.

EXHIBIT "B"

THE GENERAL ASSEMBLY OF PENNSYLVANIA
SENATE BILL NO. 1389
Session of 1986

The General Assembly makes the following findings as a basis for this act:

(1) The rapid development in recent years of interstate operations of financial institutions can be expected to continue and to have significant effects on the business of savings banks in this Commonwealth by reason of the economic, regulatory, financial and technological forces that affect the business.

(2) It is in the best interests of the economy of this Commonwealth and its public to enable savings banks in this Commonwealth to remain sound, strong and competitive with financial institutions located elsewhere.

(3) As an increasing number of states authorize financial institutions in their states to conduct interstate operations in some form, savings banks and their holding companies in this Commonwealth would be disadvantaged if not permitted to branch in any location and to combine on a regional, reciprocal basis with thrift institutions in other states.

(4) Geographic limitations on interstate operations by thrift institutions are important to the competitiveness, safety and soundness of Pennsylvania's thrift institutions.

The General Assembly of the Commonwealth of Pennsylvania hereby enacts as follows:

Section 1. Section 102 (F), (G), (I) and (X) of the Act of November 30, 1965 (P.L. 847, No. 356), known as The Banking Code of 1965, amended April 8, 1982 (P.L. 262, No. 79), are amended to read:

Section 102. Definitions

Subject to additional definitions contained in subsequent chapters of this Act which are applicable to specific chapters or sections thereof, the following words and phrases when used in this Act shall have, unless the context clearly indicates otherwise, the meanings given to them in this Section:

(F) "Bank" — A corporation which exists under the laws of this Commonwealth and, as a bank under the Banking Code of 1933, was authorized to engage in the business of receiving demand deposits on the effective date of this Act, or which receives authority to engage in such business *as a bank* pursuant to this Act, but which is not authorized to act as fiduciary.

(G) "Bank and Trust Company" — A corporation which exists under the laws of this Commonwealth and, as a bank and trust company under the Banking Code of 1933, was authorized to engage in the business of receiving demand deposits and to act as fiduciary on the effective date of this Act, or which receives authority both to engage in such business and to act as fiduciary as a bank and trust company pursuant to this Act.

(I) "Capital" — The sum of the par value of the [preferred and common] issued and outstanding shares of an institution [issued and outstanding] having a par value and the consideration received by an institution for the issued and outstanding shares of the institution without par value except such part thereof as may have been allocated other than to capital, but not in an amount greater than the amount, if any, by which:

(I) The total assets of the institution which would properly be shown on its balance sheet, exclusive of amounts due on unpaid subscriptions for shares, exceed

(II) The total of the items which would properly be shown on the liability side of its balance sheet other than such sum of the par value of its shares.

(X) "Savings Bank" — A corporation with or without capital stock which exists under the laws of this Commonwealth and as a savings bank under the Banking Code of 1933 was authorized to engage in the business of receiving savings deposits on the effective date of this Act or which receives authority to engage in such business as a savings bank pursuant to this Act.

Section 2. Section 105(a) of the Act, amended July 25, 1977 (P.L 101, No. 37), is amended to read:

Section 105. Persons Authorized to Engage in Business of Receiving Deposits and Money for Transmission

(a) Restriction of authorized persons — No person may lawfully engage in this Commonwealth in the business of receiving money for deposit or transmission, or lawfully establish in this Commonwealth a place of business for such purpose, except a bank, a bank and trust company, a savings bank, a private bank, a savings association to the extent provided in the Savings Association Code of 1967, a regional thrift institution to the extent provided in Section 117 of this Act or Section 114 of the Savings Association Code of 1967 and a person duly authorized by Federal law to engage in the business of receiving money for deposit or transmission. A bank, a bank and trust company and a savings bank that receives money for deposit shall insure such deposits with the Federal Deposit Insurance Corporation or any other Federal agency authorized by law to insure deposits.

Section 3. The Act is amended by adding sections to read:

Section 112.1. Prohibition Against Certain Acquisitions

(a) Certain acquisitions unlawful — Except as provided in Section 117, it shall be unlawful for a commercial bank, a bank holding company, a thrift institution, or a thrift institution holding company to acquire a savings bank unless the acquiring entity, and any savings and loan holding company or bank holding company which directly or indirectly owns or controls the power to vote five percent or more of its shares, is located in Pennsylvania.

(b) Definitions — The terms in subsection (a) shall have the same meaning as those terms have in Section 117.

(c) Prior acquisitions — The prohibition in subsection (a) shall not affect any acquisition effected prior to the effective date of this Act.

Section 117. Authorization of Regional, Reciprocal Operations of Savings Banks

(a) Definitions for purpose of section — The following words and phrases when used in this section shall have, unless the context clearly indicates otherwise, the following meanings:

(i) "Acquire" — to acquire (as defined in Section 112(a)(i)) five percent or more of the voting stock of an entity and shall also mean a merger or consolidation or a purchase of assets and an assumption of liabilities, other than in the regular course of business.

(ii) "Bank holding company" — the same meaning as that term has under the Bank Holding Company Act of 1956, 12 U.S.C. §1841(a).

(iii) "Branch" — an office which performs the functions described in Section 102(h).

(iv) "Control" — the power, directly or indirectly, to direct the management or policies of an entity or to vote twenty-five percent or more of any class of voting securities of an entity.

(v) "Entity" — any corporation, partnership, association or similar organization, including banks and thrift institutions.

(vi) "Pennsylvania savings bank" — a savings bank as defined in Section 102(x).

(vii) "Pennsylvania savings bank holding company" — an entity which controls one or more Pennsylvania savings banks and is located in Pennsylvania.

(viii) "Region" — the States of Delaware, Kentucky, Maryland, New Jersey, Ohio, Virginia and West Virginia, and the District of Columbia.

(ix) "Regional association" — a savings and loan association or building and loan association located in and organized and operating under the laws of a state in the region and a Federal association, as defined in 12 U.S.C. §1462(d), that is located in the region.

(x) "Regional savings bank" — a savings bank located in and organized and operating under the laws of a state in the region.

(xi) "Regional thrift institution" — a regional savings bank or a regional association.

(xii) "Regional thrift institution holding company" — an entity which controls one or more regional thrift institutions and is located in a state in the region.

(xiii) "Savings and loan holding company" — as defined in 12 U.S.C. § 1730a(a)(1)(D).

(xiv) "State" — includes the District of Columbia.

(xv) State in which an entity is "located" —

(A) with regard to a thrift institution, the state in which its deposits are largest; and

(B) with regard to a thrift institution holding company, a savings bank holding company, a savings and loan holding company or a bank holding company, the state in which the total deposits of its subsidiaries, including commercial banks, are largest.

Provided, that an entity or its legal successor that is located in Pennsylvania on the effective date of this legislation shall be deemed thereafter to be located in Pennsylvania regardless of the location of its deposits or the deposits of its subsidiaries if said entity has not been either acquired by an entity located outside of Pennsylvania or a party to a merger or consolidation transaction in which the holders of its voting shares immediately prior to the transaction hold less than fifty percent of the voting shares of any class of stock in the entity surviving after, or resulting from, the merger or consolidation.

(b) Acquisitions by regional thrift institutions and regional thrift institution holding companies — A regional thrift institution or regional thrift institution holding company may acquire a Pennsylvania savings bank or a Pennsylvania savings bank holding company if:

(i) the law of the state where the acquiring thrift institution or thrift institution holding company is located and the law of the state where any savings and loan holding company or bank holding company which directly or indirectly owns or controls the power to vote five percent or more of its shares is located satisfies, in each case, the reciprocity requirement of subsection (d);

(ii) the acquiring thrift institution or thrift institution holding company and any savings and loan holding company or bank holding company which directly or indirectly owns or controls the power to vote five percent or more of its shares is, in each case, located in a state in the region or in Pennsylvania; and

(iii) approval has been received from the department. When considering a proposed acquisition by a regional thrift institution or a regional thrift institution holding company, the department shall give specific attention to the effect of the acquisition on the availability, in this Commonwealth, of those banking and basic transaction account services set forth in subsections (i) and (j).

(c) Branching by regional savings banks —

(i) a regional savings bank may, with the prior written approval of the department, maintain as a branch any office acquired as part of an acquisition effected under this section or Section 114 of the Savings Association Code of 1967.

(ii) A regional savings bank may establish and maintain branches in this Commonwealth if:

(A) the state in which it is located, and the state in which any savings and loan holding company or bank holding company which directly or indirectly owns or has the power to vote five percent or more of its shares is located satisfies, in each case, the reciprocity requirement of subsection (d);

(B) the savings bank and any savings and loan holding company or bank holding company which directly or indirectly owns or controls the power to vote five percent or more of its shares is, in each case, located in a state in the region or in Pennsylvania; and

(C) the branch is approved by the department in the same manner and subject to the same conditions as are applicable to de novo branches of Pennsylvania savings banks under Sections 904 and 905.

(d) Reciprocity requirement —

(i) the law of another state is reciprocal under this section to the extent the department determines it to be so. The department's determination under this subsection shall include, but is not limited to:

(A) with regard to acquisitions, whether the law of that other state authorizes Pennsylvania savings banks and Pennsylvania savings bank holding companies to acquire regional thrift institutions and regional thrift institution holding companies located in that state on terms and conditions reasonably equivalent to those applicable to acquisitions by regional thrift institutions and regional thrift institution holding companies of Pennsylvania savings banks or Pennsylvania savings bank holding companies and whether the law of that other state imposes conditions on the acquisition by Pennsylvania savings banks or Pennsylvania savings bank holding companies of regional thrift institutions or regional thrift institution holding companies located in that state that are substantially more onerous than those imposed on the same acquisitions by thrift institutions or thrift institution holding companies located in that state; and

(B) with regard to branching, whether the law of that other state authorizes Pennsylvania savings banks to establish or maintain branches in that state on terms and conditions reasonably equivalent to those applicable to the establishment or maintenance of branches in Pennsylvania by savings banks located in that state, and reasonably equivalent to those applicable to the establishment and maintenance of branches in that state by a savings bank located in that state.

(ii) The department need not determine that the law of another state fails to meet the reciprocity requirement of this subsection solely by reason of the fact that that law does not allow Pennsylvania savings banks or Pennsylvania savings bank holding companies to engage in a particular type of branching or acquisition, or imposes conditions on such branching or acquisition that are substantially more onerous than those imposed on the same activities of savings banks or savings banks holding companies located in that state. However, in such circumstances, the department shall find reciprocity only after imposing on the savings banks and savings bank holding companies located in that state conditions and limitations on branching and acquisitions in Pennsylvania substantially similar to those imposed on branching and acquisitions in that state by Pennsylvania savings banks and savings bank holding companies.

(iii) The department may determine that the law of another state is not reciprocal regarding a particular type of branching or acquisition if the law of that other state does not allow all Pennsylvania savings banks or, alternatively, all Pennsylvania savings bank holding companies to engage on equal terms with each other in the particular type of branching or acquisition.

(e) Authority of the department — In addition to the powers granted elsewhere in this section and in other provisions of Pennsylvania law, the department is authorized to impose any conditions or requirements it deems appropriate, in light of the purposes of this Act, on thrift institutions and thrift institution holding companies acquired or operating directly or indirectly in Pennsylvania under this section. Such conditions or requirements include, but are not limited to, provisions for examinations, reports and the payment of fees. The department may accept examinations and other reports of Federal and state regulators and may enter into agreements with Federal and state regulators for the exchange of information, including examination reports.

(f) Change in circumstances — If a regional thrift institution or regional thrift institution holding company located in another state which has acquired a Pennsylvania savings bank or Pennsylvania savings bank holding company or has established a branch in Pennsylvania under this section shall have a change of circumstances so that it no longer satisfies the conditions of subsections (b) and (c) (either by reason of a change in the place in which it is located or by reason of acquisition by a savings and loan holding company or a bank holding company located in a state which does not satisfy the conditions of subsections (b) and (c) of five percent or more of its voting shares, or the power to vote those shares) said regional thrift institution or regional thrift institution holding company shall divest each Pennsylvania savings bank, savings bank holding company, and branch it has acquired or established prior to entering into a voluntary combination which causes such change of circumstances or within one year (or such longer period of not more than an additional year as the department may allow in writing) after the occurrence of an event, other than a voluntary combination, which causes the change in circumstances.

(g) Effect of invalidity — The purpose of this section is solely to authorize reciprocal, regional operations by savings banks and associations and this section shall not be construed to authorize any acquisition or the establishment of any branch by any entity located in another state except as expressly provided in this section. In the event that any limitation on the geographical location of entities granted acquisition or branching powers by this section is held to be invalid by a final order of a court which is not subject to further review or appeal, the authorization of this section shall terminate immediately. Any acquisition or branch establishment consummated pursuant to this section prior to such termination shall not be affected thereby.

(h) Acquisitions in other states by Pennsylvania savings banks and Pennsylvania savings bank holding companies — A Pennsylvania savings bank or Pennsylvania savings bank holding company which proposes to acquire a thrift institution or thrift institution holding company located in another state shall file an application for approval by the department in such form and upon payment of such fee as the department shall prescribe and shall supplement such application with such additional information as the department may reasonably request. The department shall conduct such investigation as it deems necessary to determine whether to approve or disapprove the application. The investigation shall include consideration of the effects the proposed acquisition would have on the availability, in this Commonwealth, of those banking services and basic transaction account services set forth in subsections (i) and (j). Within sixty days after receipt of the application or within a longer period, not in excess of thirty days after receipt from the applicant of additional information requested by the department, the department shall approve or disapprove the proposed acquisition and give written notice of its decision to the applicant. In approving an acquisition under this section, the department may place conditions upon such approval and incorporate such terms and agreements as are deemed necessary to effect the purposes of this Act.

(i) Availability of banking services — The department shall have the authority to assure that interstate thrift acquisitions authorized by this section will not diminish reasonable availability of banking services to all segments of the public and economy of this Commonwealth, with special emphasis on economic development and the financing of enterprises to the end that employment opportunities will be either increased, or, where there is the prospect of reduction, retained. Upon receipt of an application for approval of an acquisition by an institution or company located in another state under subsection (b) or approval of an acquisition in another state by a Pennsylvania savings bank or savings bank holding company under subsection (h), the department shall review the credit practices and policies of each Pennsylvania savings bank or savings bank holding company which is involved in the proposed transaction. Such review shall determine the overall performance of such company or institution in providing credit and financial services to individuals and business enterprises in the communities which it serves in the light of its role as a thrift institution, its resources, its capital and its income, the particular needs of such communities, competition and alternative sources of credit. With respect to individuals, there shall be a review of consumer loans, residential mortgages, home improvement loans and student loans, particularly to residents of low-income and moderate-income neighborhoods. With respect to business enterprises, there shall be a review of extensions of credit and investments intended to promote economic development and creation, or retention where there is the prospect of reduction, of employment opportunities, including, without limitation, small business administration and other small business loans, industrial development loans, financing of employee stock option plans and leveraged buyouts of businesses by employees, financing of nonprofit community development projects, loans and investments intended to maintain existing businesses and to encourage economic expansion and job opportunities, and loans and investments to promote participation by businesses in this Commonwealth in international trade and to increase exports. The review by the department shall also include all other activities of the institution or company deemed to be suitable to its particular circumstances and the communities served. If the department determines that the overall performance of the institution or company has not been materially deficient and that it justifies the conclusion that the institution or company does and will provide suitable credit and financial services to its communities, it may approve the application without imposing any terms or conditions but otherwise may impose such terms and conditions as it deems appropriate to improve such overall performance over a stated period of time. The department shall, from time to time, review the continuing overall performance of each such institution or company after an acquisition and, if it finds that its overall performance has not continued to be satisfactory, shall issue such order to the applicant as it deems appropriate.

(j) Availability of basic transaction account services — The department shall have the authority to assure that thrift institution holding companies and thrift institutions that become part of interstate banking organizations by reason of acquisitions requiring approval under this section make basic transaction account services available to the public. For this purpose the department shall obtain, from all sources available to it or through such studies as it may commission, adequate information to determine:

(i) The needs of the public and, in particular, individuals with low or moderate income, for a basic checking or other transaction account.

(ii) The principal characteristics that such an account should have, such as the number of checks, deposits and other items for which a minimum charge may be made, the amount or rate of such minimum charge, and the forms of identification that may be required for opening and using such an account.

(iii) The existing availability of basic accounts with some or all of such principal characteristics currently offered by depository institutions, including applicants under this section, in separate communities of this Commonwealth.

An applicant shall, at the request of the department, supply information to the department with respect to such accounts offered by the applicant and by each institution which is a subsidiary of the applicant. The department may approve an application prior to the time it has acquired the information required by this section, but the applicant and each institution which is a subsidiary of the applicant shall be subject, both before and after an approval of the acquisition under this section, to requirements imposed by the department, from time to time, to assure to the public, in the communities served by the institution, the continuing availability of the basic transaction account services which the department has determined the public needs.

(k) Advisory commission — For the purpose of advising the department in the conduct of its functions under subsections (i) and (j), the advisory commission established by Section 116(k) is empowered and directed to provide information, opinions and recommendations as to guidelines the department may establish, from time to time, for the purpose of determining the overall performance of an institution or company under subsection (i) and the availability of basic transaction account services under subsection (j). All decisions and determinations made under this section shall be made by the department.

Section 206. Interested directors and shareholders; quorum

a. Voting requirements — Any transaction authorized under Chapter 16 of this Act between an institution or subsidiary thereof and a shareholder of such an institution, or any transaction authorized under Section 1803 of this Act in which a shareholder is treated differently from other shareholders of the same class (other than any dissenting shareholders under Section 1607 of this Act), shall require the affirmative vote of the shareholders entitled to cast at least a majority of the votes which all shareholders other than the interested shareholder are entitled to cast with respect to the transaction, without counting the vote of the interested shareholder. For the purposes of the preceding sentence, interested shareholder shall include the shareholder who is a party to the transaction or who is treated differently from other shareholders and any person, or group of persons, that is acting jointly or in concert with the interested shareholder and any person who, directly or indirectly, controls, is controlled by or is under common control with the interested shareholder. An interested shareholder shall not include any person who, in good faith and not for the purpose of circumventing this subsection, is an agent, bank, broker, nominee or trustee for one or more other persons, to the extent that such other person or persons are not interested shareholders.

(b) Exceptions — subsection (a) shall not apply to a transaction:

(i) Which has been approved by a majority vote of the board of directors or trustees without counting the vote of directors or trustees who:

(A) Are directors, trustees or officers of, or have a material equity interest in, the interested shareholder; or

(B)(i) Were nominated for election as a director or trustee by the interested shareholder, and first elected as a director or trustee, within twenty-four months of the date of the vote on the proposed transaction; or (ii) in which the transaction to be received by the shareholders for shares of any class of which shares are owned by the interested shareholder is not less than the highest amount paid by the interested shareholder in acquiring shares of the same class.

(c) Approvals required — The approvals required by this section shall be in addition to, and not in lieu of, any other approval required by this Act, the articles of the institution, the bylaws of the institution or otherwise.

Section 4. Section 503 of the Act is amended to read:

Section 503. Deposits

[A savings bank may receive money for deposit and:

(a) Provisions for withdrawal — May provide by its articles or by-laws for the terms of withdrawal thereof except that deposits may not be accepted which are legally subject to withdrawal within a period of less than fourteen days.

(b) Notice in absence of provisions — Shall repay deposits on demand after sixty days' notice in the absence of any requirement of notice in its articles, by-laws or rules or in the event of failure by the savings bank to give any notice required by this Act or by its articles, by-laws or rules.

(c) Interest — May provide by rules of the savings bank or by agreement with the depositor for payment of interest on deposits for the period of the deposit and an additional period not in excess of fifteen calendar days in any one month or such longer time as the department may provide by regulations, and

(d) Limits on deposits — May limit the aggregate amount of the deposits of any one person and may refuse any deposit or return all or any part of any deposit when it deems such action in the best interests of the savings bank.] An institution may receive money for deposit and may provide by rules of the institution or by agreement with the depositor for the terms of withdrawal thereof and for payment of interest thereon for the period of the deposit and an additional period not in excess of fifteen calendar days in any one month or such longer time as the department may provide by regulation.

Section 5. Section 904(c) of the Act, amended March 4, 1982 (P.L. 135, No. 44), is amended and the section is amended by adding a subsection to read:

Section 904. Authorization of New Branches

(c) Eight years immediately following the effective date of this Act, an institution other than a savings bank may locate branches within any county in the Commonwealth, subject to the same approval of the department as is required under subsection (b)(v).

(d) A savings bank may, from and after the effective date of this Act, establish and maintain branches within any county in the Commonwealth, or within any state of the United States or the District of Columbia, subject to the same approval of the department as is required under subsection (b)(v).

EXHIBIT "C"
SENATE BILL NO. 1390

The General Assembly makes the following findings as a basis for this act:

(1) The rapid development in recent years of interstate operations of financial institutions can be expected to continue and to have significant effects on the business of savings associations in this Commonwealth by reason of the economic, regulatory, financial and technological forces that affect the business.

(2) It is in the best interests of the economy of this Commonwealth and its public to enable savings associations in this Commonwealth to remain sound, strong and competitive with financial institutions located elsewhere.

(3) As an increasing number of states authorize financial institutions in their states to conduct interstate operations in some form, savings associations and their holding companies in this Commonwealth would be disadvantaged if not permitted to branch in any location and to combine on a regional, reciprocal basis with thrift institutions in other states.

(4) Geographical limitations on interstate operations by thrift institutions are important to the competitiveness, safety and soundness of Pennsylvania's thrift institutions.

The General Assembly of the Commonwealth of Pennsylvania hereby enacts as follows:

Section 1. The act of December 14, 1967 (P.L. 746, No. 345), known as the Savings Association Code of 1967, is amended by adding sections to read:

Section 114. Authorization of Reciprocal Regional Operations of Savings Associations.— (a) The following words and phrases when used in this section shall have, unless the context clearly indicates otherwise, the following meanings:

(1) "Acquire," to acquire (as defined in Section 212(a)(1)) five percent or more of the voting stock of an entity and shall also mean a merger or consolidation or a purchase of assets and an assumption of liabilities, other than in the regular course of business.

(2) "Bank holding company," the same meaning as that term has under the Bank Holding Company Act of 1956, 12 U.S.C. § 1841(a).

(3) "Branch," an office which performs the functions described in Section 102(5).

(4) "Control," the power, directly or indirectly, to direct the management or policies of an entity or to vote twenty-five percent or more of any class of voting securities of an entity.

(5) "Entity," any corporation, partnership, association or similar organization, including banks and thrift institutions.

(6) "Pennsylvania association," an association as defined in Section 102(3) and a Federal association, as defined in 12 U.S.C. § 1462(d), that is located in Pennsylvania.

(7) "Pennsylvania association holding company," an entity which controls one or more Pennsylvania associations and is located in Pennsylvania.

(8) "Pennsylvania savings bank," a savings bank as defined in Section 102(x) of the Banking Code of 1965.

(9) "Pennsylvania thrift institution," a Pennsylvania savings bank or a Pennsylvania association.

(10) "Pennsylvania thrift institution holding company," an entity which controls one or more Pennsylvania thrift institutions and is located in Pennsylvania.

(11) "Region," the States of Delaware, Kentucky, Maryland, New Jersey, Ohio, Virginia and West Virginia, and the District of Columbia.

(12) "Regional association," a savings and loan association or building and loan association located in and organized and operating under the laws of a state in the region and a Federal association, as defined in 12 U.S.C. § 1462(d), that is located in the region.

(13) "Regional association holding company," an entity which controls one or more regional associations and is located in a state in the region.

(14) "Regional savings bank," a savings bank located in and organized and operating under the laws of a state in the region.

(15) "Regional thrift institution," a regional savings bank or a regional association.

(16) "Regional thrift institution holding company," an entity which controls one or more regional thrift institutions and is located in a state in the region.

(17) "Savings and loan holding company," the same meaning as defined in 12 U.S.C. § 1730a(a)(1)(D).

(18) "State," includes the District of Columbia.

(19) State in which an entity is "located":

(i) with regard to a thrift institution, the state in which its deposits are largest; and

(ii) with regard to a thrift institution holding company, an association holding company, a bank holding company or a savings and loan holding company, the state in which the total deposits of its subsidiaries, including commercial banks, are largest: Provided, That an entity or its legal successor that is located in Pennsylvania on the effective date of this legislation shall be deemed thereafter to be located in Pennsylvania regardless of the location of its deposits or the deposits of its subsidiaries if said entity has not been either acquired by an entity located outside of Pennsylvania or a party to a merger or consolidation transaction in which the holders of its voting shares immediately prior to the transaction held less than fifty percent of the voting shares of any class of stock in the entity surviving after, or resulting from, the merger or consolidation.

(b) A regional thrift institution or a regional thrift institution holding company may acquire a Pennsylvania association or a Pennsylvania association holding company if:

(1) The law of the state where the acquiring thrift institution or thrift institution holding company is located and the law of the state where any bank holding company or savings and loan holding company which, directly or indirectly, owns or controls the power to vote five percent or more of its shares is located satisfies, in each case, the reciprocity requirement of the subsection (e);

(2) The acquiring thrift institution or thrift institution holding company and any bank holding company or savings and loan holding company which, directly or indirectly, owns or controls the power to vote five percent or more of its shares is, in each case, located in a state in the region or in Pennsylvania; and

(3) Approval has been received from the department, when considering a proposed acquisition by a regional thrift institution or a regional thrift institution holding company, the department shall give specific attention to the effects of the acquisition on the availability, in this commonwealth, of those banking and basic transaction account services set forth in subsections (j) and (k).

(c) A regional association may, with the prior written approval of the department, maintain as a branch any office acquired as part of an acquisition effected under this section or Section 117 of the Banking Code of 1965.

(d) A regional association may establish and maintain branches in this Commonwealth if:

(1) The state in which the association is located and the state in which any bank holding company or savings and loan holding company which, directly or indirectly, owns or has the power to vote five percent or more of its shares is located satisfies, in each case, the reciprocity requirement of subsection (e);

(2) The association and any bank holding company or savings and loan company which, directly or indirectly, owns or controls the power to vote five percent or more of its shares is, in each case, located in a state in the region or in Pennsylvania; and

(3) The branch is approved by the department in the same manner, and subject to the same conditions as are applicable to, *de novo* branches of Pennsylvania associations under Sections 403 and 404.

(e) (1) The law of another state is reciprocal under this section to the extent the department determines it to be so. The department's determination under this subsection shall include, but is not limited to:

(i) with regard to acquisitions, whether the law of that other state authorizes Pennsylvania associations and Pennsylvania association holding companies to acquire regional thrift institutions and regional thrift institution holding companies located in that state on terms and conditions reasonably equivalent to those applicable to acquisitions by regional thrift institutions and regional thrift institution holding companies of Pennsylvania associations or Pennsylvania association holding companies and whether the law of that other state imposes conditions on the acquisition by Pennsylvania associations or Pennsylvania association holding companies of regional thrift institutions or regional thrift institution holding companies located in that state that are substantially more onerous than those imposed on the same acquisitions by thrift institutions or thrift institution holding companies located in that state; and

(ii) with regard to branching, whether the law of that other state authorizes Pennsylvania associations to establish or maintain branches in that state on terms and conditions reasonably equivalent to those applicable to the establishment or maintenance of branches in Pennsylvania by associations located in that state and on terms and conditions reasonably equivalent to those applicable to the establishment of branches in that state by an association located in that state.

(2) The department need not determine that the law of another state fails to meet the reciprocity requirement of this section solely by reason of the fact that that law does not allow Pennsylvania associations or Pennsylvania association holding companies to engage in a particular type of branching or acquisition or imposes conditions on such branching or acquisition that are substantially more onerous than those imposed on the same activities of thrift institutions or thrift institution holding companies located in that state. However, in such circumstances, the department shall find reciprocity only after imposing on the thrift institutions and thrift institution holding companies located in that state conditions and limitations on branching and acquisitions in Pennsylvania substantially similar to those imposed on branching and acquisitions in that state by Pennsylvania associations and association holding companies.

(3) The department may determine that the law of another state is not reciprocal regarding a particular type of branching or acquisition if the law of that other state does not allow all Pennsylvania associations or, alternatively, all Pennsylvania association holding companies to engage on equal terms with each other in the particular type of branching or acquisition. The department shall determine that the law of another state is not reciprocal regarding a particular type of branching or acquisition if the law of that other state does not allow federally chartered Pennsylvania associations (or federally chartered Pennsylvania associations converted from State-chartered Pennsylvania associations or Pennsylvania savings banks) or their holding companies to engage in the particular type of branching or acquisition on equal terms with State-chartered Pennsylvania associations or their holding companies.

(f) In addition to the powers granted elsewhere in this section and in other provisions of Pennsylvania law, the department is authorized to impose any conditions or requirements it deems appropriate, in light of the purposes of this act, on thrift institutions and thrift institution holding companies acquired or operating, directly or indirectly, in Pennsylvania under this section. Such conditions or requirements include, but are not limited to, provisions for examinations, reports and the payment of fees. The department may accept examinations and other reports of Federal and state regulators and may enter into agreements with Federal and state regulators for the exchange of information, including examination reports.

(g) If a regional thrift institution or regional thrift institution holding company located in another state which has acquired a Pennsylvania association or a Pennsylvania association holding company or has established a branch in Pennsylvania under this section shall have a change of circumstances so that it no longer satisfies the conditions of subsections (b) and (c) (either by reason of a change in the place in which it is located or by reason of acquisition by a bank holding company or a savings and loan holding company located in a state which does not satisfy the conditions of subsection (b) or (c) of five percent or more of its voting shares, or the power to vote those shares) said regional thrift institution or regional thrift institution holding company shall divest each Pennsylvania association, association holding company and branch it has acquired or established prior to entering into a voluntary combination which causes such change of circumstances or within one year (or such longer period of not more than an additional year as the department may allow, in writing) after the occurrence of an event other than a voluntary combination, which causes the change in circumstances.

(h) The purpose of this section is solely to authorize regional, reciprocal operations by associations and savings banks, and this section shall not be construed to authorize any acquisition or the establishment of any branch by any entity located in another state except as expressly provided in this section. In the event that any limitation on the geographical location of entities granted acquisition or branching powers by this section is held to be invalid by a final order of a court which is not subject to further review or appeal, the authorization of this section shall terminate immediately. Any acquisition or branch establishment consummated pursuant to this section prior to such termination shall not be affected thereby.

(i) A Pennsylvania association or Pennsylvania association holding company which proposes to acquire a thrift institution or thrift institution holding company located in another state shall file an application for approval by the department in such form and upon payment of such fee as the department shall prescribe and shall supplement such application with such additional information as the department may reasonably request. The department shall conduct such investigation as it deems necessary to determine whether to approve or disapprove the application. The investigation shall include consideration of the effects the proposed acquisition would have on the availability, in this Commonwealth, of those banking services and basic transaction account services set forth in subsections (j) and (k). Within sixty days after receipt of the application or within a longer period, not in excess of thirty days, after receipt from the applicant of additional information requested by the department, the department shall approve or disapprove the proposed acquisition and give written notice of its decision to the applicant. In approving an acquisition under this section, the department may place conditions upon such approval and incorporate such terms and agreements as are deemed necessary to effect the purposes of this act.

(j) The department shall have the authority to assure that interstate thrift acquisitions authorized by this section will not diminish reasonable availability of banking services to all segments of the public and economy of this Commonwealth, with special emphasis on economic development and the financing of enterprises to the end that employment opportunities will be either increased or, where there is the prospect of reduction, retained. Upon receipt of an application for approval of an acquisition by a company located in another state under subsection (b) or approval of an acquisition in another state by a Pennsylvania association or Pennsylvania association holding company under subsection (i), the department shall review the credit practices and policies of each Pennsylvania association or Pennsylvania association holding company which is involved in the proposed transaction. Such review shall determine the overall performance of such company or institution in providing credit and financial services to individuals and business enterprises in the communities which it serves in the light of its role as a thrift institution, its resources, its capital and its income, the particular needs of such communities, competition and alternative sources of credit. With respect to individuals, there shall be a review of consumer loans, residential mortgages, home improvement loans and student loans, particularly to residents of low-income and moderate-income neighborhoods. With respect to business enterprises, there shall be a review of extensions of credit and investments intended to promote economic development and creation, or retention where there is the prospect of reduction, of employment opportunities, including, without limitation, Small Business Administration and other small business loans, industrial development loans, financing of employee stock option plans and leveraged buy-outs of businesses by employees, financing of non-profit community development projects, loans and investments intended to maintain existing businesses and to encourage economic expansion and job opportunities, and loans and investments to promote participation by businesses in this Commonwealth in international trade and to increase exports. The review by the department shall also include all other activities of the institution or company deemed to be suitable to its particular circumstances and the communities served. If the department determines that the overall performance of the institution or company has not been materially deficient and that it justifies the conclusion that the institution or company does and will provide suitable credit and financial services to its communities, it may approve the application without imposing any terms or conditions but otherwise may impose such terms and conditions as it deems appropriate to improve such overall performance over a stated period of time. The department shall, from time to time, review the continuing overall performance of each such institution or company after an acquisition and, if it finds that its overall performance has not continued to be satisfactory, shall issue such order to the applicant as it deems appropriate.

(k) The department shall have the authority to assure that thrift institution holding companies and thrift institutions that become part of interstate banking organizations by reason of acquisitions requiring approval under this section make basic transaction account services available to the public. For this purpose the department shall obtain, from all sources available to it or through such studies as it may commission, adequate information to determine:

(1) The needs of the public and, in particular, individuals with low or moderate income, for a basic checking or other transaction account.

(2) The principal characteristics that such an account should have, such as the number of checks, deposits and other items for which a minimum charge may be made, the amount or rate of such minimum charge, and the forms of identification that may be required for opening and using such an account.

(3) The existing availability of basic accounts with some or all of such principal characteristics currently offered by depository institutions, including applicants under this section, in separate communities of the Commonwealth. An applicant shall, at the request of the department, supply information to the department with respect to such accounts offered by the applicant and by each institution which is a subsidiary of the applicant. The department may approve an application prior to the time it has acquired the information required by this section, but the applicant and each institution which is a subsidiary of the applicant shall be subject, both before and after an approval of the acquisition under this section, to requirements imposed by the department, from time to time, to assure to the public, in the communities served by the institution, the continuing availability of the basic transaction account services which the department has determined the public needs.

(1) For the purpose of advising the department in the conduct of its functions under Subsections (j) and (k), the Advisory Commission established by Section 116(k) of the Act of November 30, 1965 (P.L. 847), No. 356), known as the "Banking Code of 1965," is empowered and directed to provide information, opinions and recommendations as to guidelines the department may establish, from time to time, for the purpose of determining the overall performance of an institution or company under subsection (j) and the availability of basic transaction account services under subsection (k). All decisions and determinations made under this section shall be made by the department.

Section 212.1. Prohibition Against Certain Acquisitions.

(a) Except as provided in Section 114, it shall be unlawful for a commercial bank, a bank holding company, a thrift institution, or a thrift institution holding company to acquire a Pennsylvania association unless the acquiring entity, and any savings and loan holding company or bank holding company which directly or indirectly owns or controls the power to vote five percent or more of its shares, is located in Pennsylvania.

(b) The terms in subsection (a) shall have the same definitions as those terms have in Section 114.

(c) The prohibition in subsection (a) shall not affect any acquisition effected prior to the effective date of this Act.

Section 2. Section 403(b) of the Act, amended April 9, 1982 (P.L. 334, No. 94), is amended to read:

Section 403. Authorization of New Branches. —

(b) Except as provided in subsection (a) of this section, an association may establish a branch after the effective date of this Act anywhere in Pennsylvania and anywhere in the United States upon compliance with the following requirements:

(1) The proposed branch shall be authorized by resolution by its board of directors.

(2) If the location of the proposed branch is outside of the city, incorporated town, borough or township in which the principal place of business of the association is located, the association shall give notice of the filing of the application by advertisement in the county in which the proposed branch is to be located.

(3) The branch shall be approved by the department.

Section 3. Section 922 of the Act is amended by adding a clause to read:

Section 922. Securities and Obligations. — An association may invest its funds:

(s) With the prior approval of the department, in up to one hundred percent of the stock of a bank, a bank and trust company, a trust company, a bank holding company, a savings bank, a regional thrift institution or a regional thrift institution holding company as those terms are defined in the Banking Code of 1965 and in Section 114.

Section 4. Section 1101 of the Act is amended by adding a subsection to read:

Section 1101. Mergers, Consolidations and Conversions. —

(b.1) Upon compliance with the requirements of this article, one or more associations may merge or consolidate with a regional thrift institution as defined in, and subject to any applicable limits of, Section 114.

Section 5. Section 1301(a) of the Act is amended to read:

Section 1301. Foreign Corporation. — (a) [Foreign] Except as provided in Section 114, foreign corporations shall not transact the business of an association within this Commonwealth, nor maintain an office within this Commonwealth for the purpose of transacting such business. It shall be unlawful for any person to engage in the business of soliciting or receiving within this Commonwealth subscriptions to the shares or savings accounts of such corporations or payments therefor, or of granting loans within this Commonwealth on behalf of such corporations, or of soliciting applications therefor, or of receiving within this Commonwealth on behalf of such corporations, interest, premiums, fees or payments of any kind or of transacting business in any manner within this Commonwealth on behalf of such corporation.

Section 6. All acts and parts of acts are repealed insofar as they are inconsistent with this Act.

Section 7. This Act shall take effect in 60 days.

EXHIBIT "D"

FEDERAL HOME LOAN BANK BOARD
12 CFR Part 556
[No. 86-424]
Interstate Branching
Date: April 24, 1986.

Agency: Federal Home Loan Bank Board.

Action: Final rule with request for comments.

Summary: The Federal Home Loan Bank Board ("Board") is amending its statement of policy on branching by Federal savings and loan associations and Federal savings banks ("Federal associations") to provide: (1) General equality of Federal associations with state-chartered thrift institutions of a Federal association's home office state with respect to branching across state lines and (2) possibly broader branching rights for a Federal association acquiring a failing institution in the form of regional branching rights as well as single target state branching rights. The Board is also soliciting comments on further amending its statement of policy to provide general equality of Federal associations with state-chartered financial institutions, including banks, or their holding companies with respect to branching and acquisitions.

Dates: The rule becomes effective May 5, 1986. Comments concerning branching or acquisition equality with banks and bank holding companies must be received before August 4, 1986.

For Further Information Contact:

Winifred Sutton, Attorney, Blue Division (202) 377-7044; David Wall, Attorney, Red Division (202) 377-7397; or Mary Rawlings-Milton, Chief Paralegal, Federal Savings and Loan Insurance Corporation Attorneys Group, (202) 377-7048, Office of the General Counsel, Federal Home Loan Bank Board, 1700 G Street, N.W., Washington, D.C. 20552.

Authority

The Board is authorized to regulate the operations of Federal associations by Section 5 of the Home Owners' Loan Act of 1933, as amended ("HOLA"), 12 U.S.C. §1464 (1982 & Supp. II 1984), and it has regulated the branching of Federal associations under this authority. The Board's authority in this respect is plenary and not bounded by any restrictions of state law, and it is clear that the Board may authorize Federal associations to branch or acquire other federal associations by merger across state lines. IBAA v. FHLBB, 557 F. Supp. 23 (D.D.C. 1982).

Section 334 of the Garn-St. Germain Act added a new subsection (r) to Section 5 of the HOLA, 12 U.S.C. §1464(r) (1982), which recognized and confirmed the Board's authority to authorize interstate branching for Federal associations, but imposed a requirement that, with certain specific exceptions, any such Federal association branching across state lines must qualify as a domestic building and loan association under the Internal Revenue Code and meet the Code's asset composition test.

The case law and Section 5(r) confirm the Board's authority in this area and clearly contradict the assertions of those commenters who challenged the legal basis of such authority.

Background

The Board permitted Federal associations to branch well before the publication of its first policy statement on branching in 1967, 32 FR 20630 (Dec. 21, 1967). The Board generally limited Federal associations to branching within the states of their home offices, however, until the issuance of an amendment to its statement of policy, Board Resolution No. 81-157, 46 FR 19221 (March 30, 1981), to provide for interstate branch operations that resulted from certain supervisory acquisitions. The Board resolution provided in part:

The scope of the interstate branching prohibition in Section 556.5(a)(3) is qualified by the word "generally," which reserves to the Board discretion to approve interstate branch operations in special circumstances. The exceptional nature of acquisition transactions supervised by the Federal Savings and Loan Insurance Corporation (FSLIC) to prevent the failure of an insured institution gives rise to such special circumstances. Though the Board has authority to approve interstate acquisitions in supervisory cases, the Board's regulations do not presently set forth any policy guidelines regarding factors it will consider when deciding whether to exercise this authority.

This resolution amends the Board's policy statement to clarify that the Board may approve a merger, consolidation, or purchase of assets involving a Federal association that would not otherwise be permissible under the general rule if (1) the proposed acquisition will be effected pursuant to a plan to prevent the failure of an institution insured by the FSLIC, (2) the Board determines that the insurance liability or risk of the FSLIC will be reduced as a result of the proposed acquisition, and (3) the Board determines that the insurance liability or risk of the FSLIC resulting from the proposed acquisition transaction will be substantially less than the liability or risk that would result from otherwise equally desirable acquisition alternatives, if any, that would not result in interstate branch operations.

. . . It should be noted that the amendment accomplished by this Resolution applies only to the specific types of supervisory cases described therein. This final rule does not alter the Board's policy regarding interstate branching in non-supervisory contexts. With respect to supervisory cases to which the rule applies, the amendment does not alter the Board's long-standing preference for intrastate supervisory mergers and acquisitions.

The policy statement on interstate branching has been amended since the issuance of Resolution No. 81-157, by Resolution Nos. 81-496, 46 FR 45120 (Oct. 10, 1981), and 82-498, 47 FR 34125 (Aug. 6, 1982), but such amendments have clarified the original policy statement without altering its basic purposes and limitations. A proposed rule that would have enlarged the scope of interstate branching and acquisition by all institutions the accounts of which are insured by the Federal Savings and Loan Insurance Corporation ("insured institutions") was published for notice and comment in 1983, but was not adopted. Board Resolution No. 83-244, 48 FR 20930 (May 10, 1983).

The Board has also adopted a final rule concerning branching across state lines within the region formed by the District of Columbia, Maryland, and Virginia, Board Resolution No. 86-423 (April 24, 1986). The amendment set forth in the present resolution is general and does not supersede the Board's specific rulemaking for that region.

It should be noted that the Board may authorize acquisitions of failing insured institutions by out of state acquirers under the temporary authority of Section 408(m) of the National Housing Act, 12 U.S.C. §1730a(m) (1982), added by Section 123 of the Garn-St. Germain Act, and the Board has employed this authority on several occasions. This extraordinary authority, which is separate from the Board's general rulemaking power over Federal association branching under Section 5 of the HOLA, will expire in the middle of July, unless extended by Congress. Pub. L. No. 99-278 (1986).

On June 10, 1985, the United States Supreme Court decided that state statutes that selectively authorized interstate branch acquisitions on a regional basis did not violate the "Douglas Amendment" to the Bank Holding Company Act or the Constitution of the United States. *Northeast Bancorp, Inc. v. Board of Governors of the Federal Reserve System*, No. 84-363 (U.S. June 10, 1985). Section 3(d) of the Bank Holding Company Act, 12 U.S.C. §1824(d) (1982), known as the "Douglas Amendment," prohibits the Board of Governors from approving an application of a bank holding company or bank located in one state to acquire a bank located in another state unless the acquisition "is specifically authorized by the statute laws of the State in which such bank is located by language to that effect and not merely by implication." From 1956 to 1972, the Douglas Amendment had the effect of barring interstate bank acquisitions because no state had enacted the requisite authorizing statutes. Beginning in 1972, some states enacted statutes permitting such acquisitions in limited circumstances or for specific purposes. Beginning with Massachusetts in 1982, several states enacted statutes authorizing interstate acquisitions on a reciprocal basis within their geographical regions. In *Northeast Bancorp*, the Supreme Court upheld Massachusetts and Connecticut statutes allowing regional acquisitions as consistent with the Douglas Amendment and the Bank Holding Company Act as a whole, and as not violating the Commerce Clause, the Compact Clause, or the Equal Protection Clause of the United States Constitution.

In regulating branching of Federal associations generally, the Board has traditionally provided Federal associations with potential branching rights as broad as those that would be provided under State law for thrifts or commercial banks in the state in which a Federal association is located (as set forth, for example, in the 1979 codification of the Board's policy statement on the organization and branching of Federal associations, at 12 CFR 556.5(b)(1)(1979)).

State law regarding interstate expansion by financial institutions can best be described in terms of emerging trends. Roughly speaking, the states fall into three categories in their articulated statutory attitudes toward interstate expansion. First, there are states that do not allow any form of interstate expansion. Second, there are a growing number that have authorized interstate expansion on a regional, often reciprocal, basis. Finally, there are states which have authorized potential entry by out of the state institutions not limited to a region. There remain, of course, a number of states that do not address this issue by statute, as well as state statutes that defy easy categorization.

There are differences among those states that permit some sort of interstate expansion by financial institutions concerning the type of institution that may branch or acquire and what form the expansion may take: merger, acquisition, establishment or de novo branches, etc. A majority permits some form of interstate expansion by banks, and at least half of those allow expansion by thrifts. Regional limitations vary considerably; some states provide for future regional expansion through reciprocity.

Most of the states that permit interstate expansion by thrifts permit entry by merger or acquisition. Maine limits entry by out of state financial institutions to the establishment of, or the acquisition of control over, a Maine financial institution or holding company by an out of state holding company.

Request for Further Comment

The Board's proposal diverged from its traditional approach to the application of state law standards to Federal association branching in that the proposed rule was more conservative, looking only to state law applicable to thrift institutions instead of that applicable to "state financial depository institutions" generally, as expressed in 12 CFR 556.5(a)(2) (1985). Upon consideration of the comments received and a review of state legislation in this area, the Board has determined that a conservative standard, looking only to state law applicable to thrift institutions, should be employed at this time as the standard for Federal association branching across state lines in a nonsupervisory context.

The Board has also decided, however, to invite further comment, for a ninety day period, upon this standard and the possibility of using other standards: state law applicable to all financial depository institutions insured by the FSLIC or the Federal Deposit Insurance Corporation, or state law applicable to such financial depository institutions and their holding companies.

Final Rule

The Board's final rule applies a thrift institution standard to determine interstate Federal association branching rights in a nonsupervisory context, as proposed, but the amendment further clarifies the proposal by providing that state law shall be looked to only with respect to basic authority to establish branch offices; approvals by state authority are not incorporated, nor are related state law investment standards or prerequisites, which would be inconsistent with a federal rule for Federal associations already subject to regulation in these matters. State law will be followed, however, in distinguishing the capacity to branch de novo from the capacity to acquire offices by merger. The amendment does not authorize a Federal association to become a savings and loan holding company.

The Board has determined to adopt the proposed special rules concerning Federal associations within a holding company structure, but has attempted to clarify these rules. In many ways, these rules embody principles explicitly or implicitly set forth in the structure of the Federal savings and loan system, the Savings and Loan Holding Company Amendments of 1967, and Board actions in which acquisition limitations of the Savings and Loan Holding Company Amendments of 1967 were overridden by the FSLIC under the temporary special authority of Section 408(m) of the National Housing Act, 12 U.S.C. §1730a(m) (1982). A Federal association that is itself the ultimate parent holding company in a holding company structure is treated, in substance, as if the other associations in the structure were its branches. Extraordinary acquisitions under temporary provisions of the Garn-St. Germain Act are not made a basis to ''leverage'' wide ranging branching authority. And the basic purposes of the Savings and Loan Holding Company Amendments are observed. In response to comments received, and subject to the limitations, the Board has determined to adopt a final rule that provides greater scope for management decision. Except for certain delineated circumstances, a Federal association would not be precluded from utilizing interstate branching rights solely because another institution in the holding company structure possessed such rights, but only if such other institution exercised such rights.

Since 1981, the Board has recognized that different rules should apply to the acquisition of branches and branching rights in connection with actions to prevent the failure of institutions, the accounts of which are insured by the FSLIC. The Board's basic policy initiative of 1981, granting interstate branching capacity in connection with the acquisition of a failing institution, preceded the Garn-St. Germain Act and was fully implemented prior to the enactment of that statute. The amended final rule is consistent with that initiative. In a context of expanding opportunities for financial institutions, represented by the growth of ''regional compacts,'' and increasing costs of FSLIC actions with respect to failing institutions, it is appropriate to modify the existing rules for the acquisition of failing institutions to provide a potential branching capacity that is more consistent with the greater opportunities now available to financial institutions and with the assistance programs of the FSLIC.

The Board continues to favor limited interstate acquisitions and branching, however, and the rule gives preference to simpler, limited applications, such as those seeking entry only into the state of a failing target institution, over those seeking wider capacity. As stated in the proposal, the amended rule merely expands the Board's flexibility under its own rules to grant branching capacity in connection with the acquisition of assets or liabilities of failing institutions and for the purpose of serving the needs of the FSLIC. It is not the Board's purpose to signal a move toward general unrestricted branching on a national or broad scale in connection with supervisory cases. The Board has considered the variations suggested by the commenters that would be within its authority, but has determined that the steps taken by the amended rule are appropriate at this time. The Board has also decided that implementation of the principles of the amended rule should proceed on a case by case basis without imposing deductive restrictions that are not based upon experience. The Board has decided, however, to clarify the rule by requiring that a grant of branching rights in states other than the state of the target must be supported by a showing that the additional branching is reasonably related to the structure of the applicant, before or after acquisition of a target institution, and that the proposed acquisition if of very substantial benefit to the FSLIC, in a measure sufficient to constitute a compelling factor in determining to make an award to the applicant.

As indicated, the amendment addresses branching capacity for Federal associations generally and in connection with the acquisition of failing institutions. The approval of particular branches remains, of course, subject to standard regulatory procedures.

The Board has determined that this amendment shall become effective immediately upon publication. In the present circumstances of the savings and loan industry, and in particular in view of the large and growing number of distressed insured institutions that are eligible for FSLIC assistance and the increasing cost to the FSLIC of delays in the marketing and acquisition of distressed institutions, it is imperative that the improvements made under this rule be effected without delay. There is no reason to expect that any person or interest will be harmed by making this rule effective upon publication. Any interested party's ability to prepare to take action or to enjoy a reasonable time in which to respond to proposed actions under the new rule would not be impaired by an immediate effective date. The benefits derived from not delaying the effective date are substantial and compelling from the standpoint of the FSLIC. Accordingly, the Board has determined that good cause exists for providing that this rule shall be effective upon publication and that such good cause satisfies the requirements of 12 CFR 508.14 (1985) and the rulemaking provisions of the Administrative Procedure Act; 5 U.S.C. §553(d) (1982).

§ 556.5 Establishment of branch offices

(a) General. (1) The Board encourages a competitive savings and loan system that provides choices of facilities for improved financial services to the public. The Board believes that branching is a primary means to increase competition and serve the public. The Board recognizes that establishment of a full service branch is only one means for improving service and competition in an area and, therefore, encourages innovative ideas for branches designed to suit the needs of a particular community.

(2) As a general policy, the Board permits a Federal association to branch within the state in which its home office is located.

(3)(i)(a)(1) Additionally, the Board will permit a Federal association to establish or operate a branch office in a state other than the state in which its home office is located if the law of the state in which a Federal association's home office is located and the law of the state in which the branch is to be located would permit the establishment of such branch if the Federal association were an institution of the savings and loan or savings bank type chartered by the state in which the Federal association's home office is located.

(2) For the purposes of this paragraph (a)(3)(i)(a), state law is employed to determine basic authority to branch, or to acquire branch offices by merger or acquisition of assets or liabilities, but authorization by a state official is not required, and other state law limitations or requirements, such as those concerning investment standards, do not apply.

(3) This paragraph (a)(3)(i)(a) does not authorize a Federal association to become a savings and loan holding company controlling an insured institution located in a state other than the state in which the Federal association's home office is located.

(b) For the purposes of this paragraph (a)(3), the home office of a Federal association shall be deemed to be its home office as of the later of the date of its chartering or December 20, 1985, unless an association clearly demonstrates to the satisfaction of the Board that relocation to another state was not effected primarily to obtain branching advantages under this §556.5(a).

(c) If a Federal association is a holding company or a subsidiary of an insured institution that is a holding company, it shall have a home office for the purposes of paragraph (a)(3)(i) only if no other insured institution in its holding company structure exercises or has exercised branching rights described in paragraph (a)(3)(i)(a);

(d) If a Federal association is an ultimate parent holding company, and no state chartered insured institution in the holding company structure exercises or has exercised branching rights described in paragraph (a)(3)(i)(a), such ultimate parent holding company shall be the sole association in the holding company structure that may acquire such branching rights under paragraph (a)(3)(i)(a). For the purposes of this paragraph (a)(3)(i), "ultimate parent holding company" means a savings and loan holding company not controlled by another company.

(e) Multiple holding companies. (1) A Federal association that is a subsidiary of a multiple savings and loan holding company that controls insured institutions located in more than one state shall have a home office for the purposes of paragraph (a)(3)(i) only if no other subsidiary insured institution of its holding company exercises or has exercised branching rights described in paragraph (a)(3)(i)(a).

(2) Such a subsidiary Federal association may not exercise branching rights described in paragraph (a)(3)(i)(a) if a single state has been designated by its parent pursuant to Section 408(e)(3)(B) of the National Housing Act, 12 U.S.C. §1730a(e)(3)(B), that is not the state in which such subsidiary Federal association has its home office, or if it became a subsidiary of its parent holding company pursuant to an acquisition or acquisitions effected pursuant to Section 408(m) of the National Housing Act at a time when that parent was an existing savings and loan holding company, unless no subsidiary of such parent in a state designated pursuant to §408(e)(3)(B) or existing prior to such Section 408(m) acquisition possesses branching rights described in paragraph (a)(3)(i)(a).

(f) A Federal association that acquires and exercises branching rights pursuant to any of subparagraphs (a)(3)(i)(a) through (e) may not operate or retain branches established pursuant to such exercise if another insured institution in its holding company structure exercises branching rights described in paragraph (a)(3)(i)(a).

(ii)(a) Notwithstanding the limitations of paragraph (a)(3)(i) of this section, but subject to Section 5(r) of the Home Owner's Loan Act of 1933, as amended, the Board may approve the establishment or operation of a branch office by a Federal association in a state other than the state in which its home office is located; Provided that:

(1) The establishment of the branch office will be achieved as part of or as a result of a transaction in which assets or liabilities of a failing insured institution ("target institution") are acquired by another institution, by merger or otherwise, as part of a transaction in which the insured accounts of a target institution are assumed by and transferred to an insured institution as a means of payment of insurance by the Federal Savings and Loan Insurance Corporation ("Corporation") or pursuant to an action by the Corporation to prevent the failure of a target institution;

(2) The Board determines that the Corporation's insurance liability or risk, including cost or potential cost to the Corporation, will be reduced as a result of the transaction involving a target institution; and

(3) If any alternative has been submitted that is not objectionable on supervisory grounds and could be approved in accordance with paragraph (a)(2), (a)(3)(i), or (a)(3)(iii) of this section or that would involve an acquisition by, or transfer of accounts to a state chartered institution and would be in accordance with the laws governing the chartering and operation of all parties to the transaction, the Board determines that the Corporation's insurance liability or risk, including cost or potential cost to the Corporation, resulting from the proposed interstate acquisition by, or transfer of accounts to, a Federal association under this paragraph (a)(3)(ii) will be substantially less than the liability or risk that would result from such other alternative.

(b) Branching approved or permitted pursuant to this paragraph (a)(3)(ii) may be:

(1) Operation of a former office or offices of a target institution; and

(2) Permission to establish branch offices in a state or states other than the state or states in which a target institution operates: Provided that branching rights permitted pursuant to this paragraph (a)(3)(ii)(b)(2) shall not in any event include any state in addition to the greater of (A) three (3) states in addition to the state or states in which the target institution operates, or (B) if the home office of the target institution is located in a state that, as of the date of acquisition of the target institution, is included in a regional compact of states specifically authorizing branching or acquisition across state lines by institutions of the savings and loan or savings bank type by statute laws of such states, by language to that effect and not merely by implication, the states included within such as regional compact; Provided further, that the Board shall give preference to an application seeking limited branching authority over an application seeking wider branching capacity under paragraphs (a)(3)(ii)(b)(1)

and (2); Provided further, that in considering applications to approve transactions involving the exercise of authority under this paragraph (a)(3)(ii)(b)(2), the Board shall prefer an application involving branching in states within a regional compact for institutions of the savings and loan or savings bank type or in a state having boundary lines contiguous with boundary lines of the state in which the target institution's home office is located; and Provided further, that no application for branching capacity under this paragraph (a)(3)(ii)(b)(2) shall be approved unless the Board finds that such branching capacity is reasonably related to the office structure of the applicant, before or after acquisition of the target institution or its assets or liabilities, and that an acquisition effected pursuant to such application is of very substantial benefit to the FSLIC in a measure sufficient to constitute a compelling factor in determining to make an award to the applicant.

(c) The principles of this paragraph (a)(3)(ii) shall also apply in reverse mergers in which the target institution is the surviving entity and in the acquisition of control of subsidiary insured institutions in a state or states in which a Federal association is not authorized to branch pursuant to paragraph (a)(3)(i).

(iii) Notwithstanding paragraph (a)(3)(i) of this section, but subject to Section 5(r) of the Home Owners' Loan Act of 1933, as amended, the Board may approve the establishment of a branch office in a state or states other than the state in which the home office is located, provided that the establishment of the branch office will be achieved by the consolidation of some or all of the savings and loan subsidiaries, or of some or all of the offices of the savings and loan subsidiaries, of a multiple savings and loan holding company. The Board may approve the establishment of a branch office by a resulting institution in any state or states in which it maintains branch offices as a result of the consolidation.

(iv) Notwithstanding paragraph (a)(3)(i) of this section, but subject to Section 5(r) or the Home Owners' Loan Act of 1933, as amended, in a transaction not involving an action by the Corporation for transfer of accounts or to prevent the failure of an insured institution, the Board may approve the establishment of a branch office in any state in which the applicant has established or has been permitted to operate a branch office pursuant to the conditions set forth in paragraph (a)(3)(ii) of this section.

EXHIBIT "E"
MCFADDEN ACT
12 U.S.C. § 36

(a) A national banking association may retain and operate such branch or branches as it may have had in lawful operation on February 25, 1927, and any national banking association which continuously maintained and operated not more than one branch for a period of more than twenty-five years immediately preceding February 25, 1927, may continue to maintain and operate such branch.

(b) (1) A national bank resulting from the conversion of a State bank may retain and operate as a branch any office which was a branch of the State bank immediately prior to conversion if such office —

(A) might be established under subsection (c) of this section as a new branch of the resulting national bank, and is approved by the Comptroller of the Currency for continued operation as a branch of the resulting national bank;

(B) was a branch of any bank on February 25, 1927; or

(C) is approved by the Comptroller of the Currency for continued operation as a branch of the resulting national bank.

The Comptroller of the Currency may not grant approval under clause (C) of this paragraph is a State bank (in a situation identical to that of the national bank) resulting from the conversion of a national bank would be prohibited by the law of such State from retaining and operating as a branch an identically situated office which was a branch of the national bank immediately prior to conversion.

(2) A national bank (referred to in this paragraph as the "resulting bank"), resulting from the consolidation of a national bank (referred to in this paragraph as the "national bank") under whose charter the consolidation is effected with another bank or banks, may retain and operate as a branch any office which, immediately prior to such consolidation, was in operation as —

(A) a main office or branch office of any bank (other than the national bank) participating in the consolidation if, under subsection (c) of this section, it might be established as a new branch of the resulting bank, and if the Comptroller of the Currency approves of its continued operation after the consolidation;

(B). a branch of any bank participating in the consolidation, and which, on February 25, 1927, was in operation as a branch of any bank; or

(C) a branch of the national bank and which, on February 25, 1927, was not in operation as a branch of any bank, if the Comptroller of the Currency approves of its continued operation after the consolidation.

The Comptroller of the Currency may not grant approval under clause (C) of this paragraph if a State bank (in a situation identical to that of the resulting national bank) resulting from the consolidation into a State bank of another bank or banks would be prohibited by the law of such State from retaining and operating as a branch an identically situated office which was a branch of the State bank immediately prior to consolidation.

(3) As used in this subsection, the term "consolidation" includes a merger.

(c) A national banking association may, with the approval of the Comptroller of the Currency, establish and operate new branches: (1) Within the limits of the City, town or village in which said association is situated, if such establishment and operation are at the time expressly authorized to State banks by the law of the State in question; and (2) at any point within the State in which said association is situated, if such establishment and operation are at the time authorized to State banks by the statute law of the State in question by language specifically granting such authority affirmatively and not merely by implication or recognition, and subject to the restrictions as to location imposed by the law of the State on State banks. In any State in which State banks are permitted by statute law to maintain branches within county or greater limits, if no bank is located and doing business in the place where the proposed agency is to be located, any national banking association situated in such State may, with the approval of the Comptroller of the Currency, establish and operate, without regard to the capital requirements of this section, a seasonal agency in any resort community within the limits of the county in which the main office of such association is located, for the purpose of receiving and paying out deposits, issuing and cashing checks and drafts, and doing business incident thereto; Provided, That any permit issued under this sentence shall be revoked upon the opening of a State or national bank in such community. Except as provided in the immediately preceding sentence, no such association shall establish a branch outside of the city, town, or village in which it is situated unless it has a combined capital stock and surplus equal to the combined amount of capital stock and surplus, if any, required by the law of the State in which such association is situated for the establishment of such branches by State banks, or, if the law of such State requires only a minimum capital stock for the establishment of such branches by State banks, unless such association has not less than an equal amount of capital stock.

(d) The aggregate capital of every national banking association and its branches shall at no time be less than the aggregate minimum capital required by law for the establishment of an equal number of national banking associations situated in the various places where such association and its branches are situated.

(e) No branch of any national banking association shall be established or moved from one location to another without first obtaining the consent and approval of the Comptroller of the Currency.

(f) The term "branch" as used in this section shall be held to include any branch bank, branch office, branch agency, additional office, or any branch place of business located in any State or Territory of the United States or in the District of Columbia at which deposits are received, or checks paid, or money lent.

(g) This section shall not be construed to amend or repeal Sections 601-605 of this title, authorizing the establishment by national banking associations of branches in foreign countries, or dependencies, or insular possessions of the United States.

(h) The words "State bank," "State banks," "bank," or "banks," as used in this section, shall be held to include trust companies, savings banks, or other such corporations or institutions carrying on the banking business under the authority of State laws. R.S. § 5155; Feb. 25, 1927, c. 191, § 7, 44 Stat. 1228; June 16, 1933, c. 89, § 23, 48 Stat. 189, 190; Aug. 23, 1935, c. 614, § 305, 49 Stat. 708.

EXHIBIT "F"
Douglas Amendment
12 U.S.C. § 1842(d)

(d) Limitation by State Boundaries

Notwithstanding any other provision of this section, no application (except an application filed as a result of a transaction authorized under Section 1823(f) of this title) shall be approved under this section which will permit any bank holding company or any subsidiary thereof to acquire, directly or indirectly, any voting shares of, interest in, or all or substantially all of the assets of any additional bank located outside of the State in which the operations of such bank holding company's banking subsidiaries were principally conducted on July 1, 1966, or the date on which such company became a bank holding company, whichever is later, unless the acquisition of such shares or assets of a State bank by an out-of-State bank holding company is specifically authorized by the statute laws of the State in which such bank is located, by language to that effect and not merely by implication. For the purposes of this section, the State in which the operations of a bank holding company's subsidiaries are principally conducted is that State in which total deposits of all such banking subsidiaries are largest.

EXHIBIT "G-1"   ISA-2

APPLICATION TO ACQUIRE CONTROL
OR 5% OR MORE OF THE VOTING SHARES OF
A PENNSYLVANIA INSTITUTION OR BANK HOLDING COMPANY

Date   333 Market St., 16th Floor
Submitted_____   Harrisburg, PA 17101-2290

Pursuant to the provisions of Section 116 of the Pennsylvania Banking Code of 1965, as amended, application is hereby made to The Secretary of Banking of the Commonwealth of Pennsylvania, for approval to acquire direct or indirect ownership, control or the power to vote at least _____ (No.) of the voting shares (_____ %) of the Pennsylvania Institution or Bank Holding Company, hereinafter referred to as the "Subject":

APPLICANT	SUBJECT
(Corporate Title)	(Corporate Title)
(Street) (City, Borough or Township)	(Street) (City, Borough or Township)
(Zip Code) (County) (State)	(Zip Code) (County) (State)
State and Date of Incorporation_____	State and Date of Incorporation_____
Number of Affiliates: Bank ____ Nonbank ____	Number of Affiliates: Bank ____ Nonbank ____

CORPORATE REPRESENTATIVE(S) RESPONSIBLE FOR RESPONDING TO QUESTIONS ON THIS APPLICATION:
  Name   Title   Address   Telephone No.

In consideration of this application for approval, the undersigned submit the following representations and supporting documentation as evidence thereof:

FIRST, that the Pennsylvania Department of Banking shall have the authority to require reports of condition from, and to examine the books, records and affairs of the Applicant and or the Subject bank or bank holding company (including affiliates thereof) in the State of its location to the extent that the Department is now empowered within the Commonwealth of Pennsylvania.

ISA-2

SECOND, that the law of the State in which the Applicant is located:

A. Is substantially no more restrictive as to the terms and conditions of acquisitions within said State by a Pennsylvania Bank Holding Company than those applied to the institutions located within that State filing like applications;

B. Does not apply restrictions on the competitive, operational powers of a Pennsylvania Bank Holding Company filing application for an acquisition which would not generally be applicable to like institutions within said State;

C. Does not impose a specified period of time that a bank must be in operation as a condition for approval of such an acquisition. (If so, give details.)

THIRD, that the regional structure of the applicant bank holding company, by total domestic deposits as defined in Section 116(a)(iv) of the Banking Code, is correctly stated as follows:

State	Before Acquisition			State	After Acquisition		
	No. of Banks	Domestic Deposits*			No. of Banks	Domestic Deposits*	
		Total	%			Total	%
		M				M	
Totals		M	100%	Totals		M	100%

*Deposit data should be as of the last semiannual Call Report - June 30 or December 31.

FOURTH, that this acquisition would be consistent with the requirements of adequate and sound banking and in the interest of the public and the economy of the Commonwealth of Pennsylvania.

ISA-2

FIFTH, that in support of these representations, the undersigned have annexed to this application those attachments listed and enumerated below incorporating expressly by reference the information set forth therein within this application:

Attachment I – Copies of the resolutions of the Board of Directors of the Applicant and Subject institution authorizing this application and the individual(s) responsible for its execution.

II – A copy of the statute(s) in the law of the State in which the Applicant is located regarding acquisitions by a bank holding company located within or outside said State.

III – A resume of the financial history (five years) and managerial background of the Applicant and Subject institution.

IV – An analysis of the competitive factors and effects of this acquisition on the Pennsylvania economic sector(s) involved.

V – Copies of the policy statements of the Applicant and of the Subject and its affiliates, as related to the Community Reinvestment Act, 12 USC 2901 et seq. and Section 116(I) of the Pennsylvania Banking Code of 1965, as amended.

VI – An outline for the provision of "Basic Transaction Account Services" in compliance with Section 116(J) of the Pennsylvania Banking Code of 1965, as amended.

We, the undersigned, do hereby solemnly swear, that the information herein contained, or hereto attached, is true and complete, to the best of our knowledge and belief.

APPLICANT	SUBJECT
By: _____	By. _____
Name/Title:	Name/Title:
Attest: _____	Attest: _____
Name/Title:	Name/Title:

EXHIBIT "G-2"　　　　　　　　　　　　　　　　　　　　　　　　　ISA-1

APPLICATION TO ACQUIRE OR CONTROL
AN OUT-OF-STATE
BANK OR BANK HOLDING COMPANY

Date　　　　　　　　　　　　　　　　　　　　　　　333 Market St., 16th Floor
Submitted_____　　　　　　　Harrisburg, PA 17101-2290

Pursuant to the provisions of Section 116 of the Pennsylvania Banking Code of 1965, as amended, application is hereby made to The Secretary of Banking of the Commonwealth of Pennsylvania, for approval to acquire direct or indirect ownership or control 25% or more of the voting shares of the Out-of-State Bank or Bank Holding Company, hereinafter referred to as the "Subject":

APPLICANT	SUBJECT
(Corporate Title)	(Corporate Title)
(Street)　　　(City, Borough or Township)	(Street)　　　(City, Borough or Township)
(Zip Code)　(County)　(State)	(Zip Code)　(County)　(State)
State and Date of Incorporation_____	State and Date of Incorporation_____
Number of Affiliates:　Bank ___　Nonbank ___	Number of Affiliates:　Bank ___　Nonbank ___

CORPORATE REPRESENTATIVE(S) RESPONSIBLE FOR RESPONDING TO QUESTIONS ON THIS APPLICATION:
　Name　　　　　　Title　　　　　　Address　　　　　　Telephone No.

In consideration of this application for approval, the undersigned submit the following representations and supporting documentation as evidence thereof:

FIRST, that the Pennsylvania Department of Banking shall have the authority to require reports of condition from, and to examine the books, records and affairs of the Applicant and of the Subject bank or bank holding company (including affiliates thereof) in the State of its location to the extent that the Department is now empowered within the Commonwealth of Pennsylvania.

ISA-1

SECOND, that the regional structure of the applicant bank holding company, by total domestic deposits as defined in Section 116(a)(iv) of the Banking Code, is correctly stated as follows:

State	Before Acquisition			State	After Acquisition		
	No. of Banks	Domestic Deposits*			No. of Banks	Domestic Deposits*	
		Total	%			Total	%
		M				M	
Totals		M	100%	Totals		M	100%

*Deposit data should be as of the last semiannual Call Report - June 30 or December 31.

THIRD, that this acquisition would be consistent with the requirements of adequate and sound banking and in the interest of the public and economy of the Commonwealth of Pennsylvania.

ISA-1

FOURTH, that in support of these representations, the undersigned have annexed to this application those attachments listed and enumerated below incorporating expressly by reference the information set forth therein within this application:

Attachment I – Copies of the resolutions of the Board of Directors of the Applicant and Subject institution authorizing this application and the individual(s) responsible for its execution.

II – A copy of the statute(s) in the law of the State in which the Subject is located regarding acquisitions by a bank holding company located within or outside said State.

III – A resume of the financial history (five years) and managerial background of the Applicant and Subject institution.

IV – An analysis of the competitive factors and effects of this acquisition on the Pennsylvania economic sector(s) involved.

V – Copies of the policy statements of the Applicant and each affiliate thereof, as related to the Community Reinvestment Act, 12 USC 2901 et seq. and Section 116(I) of the Pennsylvania Banking Code of 1965, as amended.

VI – An outline for the provision of "Basic Transaction Account Services" in compliance with Section 116(J) of the Pennsylvania Banking Code of 1965, as amended.

We, the undersigned, do hereby solemnly swear that the information herein contained, or hereto attached, is true and complete, to the best of our knowledge and belief.

APPLICANT	SUBJECT
By: _____	By: _____
Name/Title:	Name/Title:
Attest: _____	Attest: _____
Name/Title:	Name/Title:

100

EXHIBIT "G-3"

PROCEDURES AND INSTRUCTIONS FOR

APPLICATIONS FOR INTERSTATE ACQUISITIONS

FILING

APPLICATION

Complete in entirety. Failure to complete or furnish requested data will cause the application to be returned to the applicant or held by the Department for additional requested information, which will defer the original filing date to that of receipt of the completed matter.

Submit two (2) _signed_ copies of the application and supporting documentation to the Department.

FEE(S)

The fee for filing an application for an acquisition is $5,000. A check for that amount, payable to the Pennsylvania Department of Banking, must be submitted with the application.

The applicant will also be responsible for the payment of all expenses incurred in the process of conducting field investigations, where applicable.

NOTICES BY APPLICANT

Within seven (7) days of the filing of the application with the Department of Banking, the applicant shall have notice(s) published similar in format to the sample notice on Page 4, attached.

Publication of the advertisement shall be made in a newspaper of general circulation located in or serving the area of the Headquarters location of the Applicant and also the Principal Operating Office of each Subsidiary Bank, directly or indirectly owned or to be acquired.

Certified copies of said advertisement(s) must be received by the Department of Banking within ten (10) days of publication or the application shall be deemed incomplete and subject to the revision of the original filing date (Date recorded as received by the Department).

PREPARATION

The basic application is comprised of three forms, Pages 1 through 3, identifying the parties and intent thereof in fundamental representations. Detailed schedules or inserts providing the required supporting information are to be rendered with the application as attachments or exhibits, on the same size paper (8½" x 11"), properly indexed and securely bound.

Where requested on the basic forms, "Number of Affiliates" or "Banks" is construed to mean all such entities owned or controlled both directly and indirectly. The Applicant is to attach to the application a complete listing, by name and location, of all such entities of both the Applicant and Subject institutions.

In consideration of attachments III and IV, as listed under the appropriate representation on Page 3 of the application, the applicant shall submit a copy of some or all of the following documents which are pertinent to the proposed acquisition:

1. Application to the Federal Reserve Board pursuant to the Federal Bank Holding Company Act.

2. Prospectus or proxy statement distributed to shareholders pursuant to Federal securities laws and documents incorporated therein by reference.

3. Any other application filed with a Federal or state bank regulatory authority in connection with the proposed acquisition.

The Applicant bears the full burden for presenting and documenting a case to meet the statutory criteria for approval.

In consideration of Attachments IV and V regarding economic effects and Community Reinvestment Act statements, specific reference should be made to the following:

1. The effect the acquisition will have on the financing of enterprises to the end that employment opportunities will either be increased and/or retained.

2. A comparative evaluation of the overall performance of each Pennsylvania Bank Holding Company and/or Pennsylvania Institution, who is a party to this application, with their CRA statement of policy regarding credit and financial services to individuals and businesses in the communities they serve, as follows (data should be as of the last semiannual Call Report date - June 30 or December 31):

    A. With respect to loans to individuals:

    (1) The percentage of each of the following types of loans to Total Assets
    (2) The percentage of each of the following types of loans to Total Loans
    (3) The percentage of each of the following types of loans to Total Assets made in low and moderate income neighborhoods
    (4) The percentage of each of the following types of loans to Total Loans made in low and moderate income neighborhoods
    (5) Indicate the neighborhood in each instance
    (6) Types of loans:

        (a) Consumer Loans
        (b) Residential Loans
        (c) Home Improvement Loans
        (d) Student Loans

B. With respect to business loans and investments made to promote the economic development and creation or retention of employment opportunities within the Commonwealth of Pennsylvania, indicate the total amount of the following types of loans outstanding and the percentage of each type of such loans to total loans outstanding:

(1) Small Business Loans (SBA)
(2) Other Small Business Loans
(3) Industrial Development Authority Loans (IDA)
(4) Financing of Employee Stock Option Plans (ESOP)
(5) Financing of Leveraged Buyouts of Business by Employees
(6) Financing of Nonprofit Community Development Projects
(7) Loans and Investments Intended to Maintain Existing Businesses
(8) Loans and Investments to Encourage Economic Expansion and Job Opportunities
(9) Loans and Investments to Promote Participation by Businesses in this State in International Trade and to Increase Exports
(10) All Other Activities of the Pennsylvania Institution(s) Owned or to be Owned Deemed Suitable to Its Particular Circumstances and the Communities Served

Definitions for the foregoing types of loans, where applicable, may be found in the Call Report instructions issued by the Federal Financial Institutions Examination Council (FFIEC).

3. Submit a record of challenges to the CRA statements of the Applicant and Subject and all of their currently owned affiliate banks over the past five years.

In consideration of Attachment VI, the Applicant must submit information verifying that each Pennsylvania Institution currently owned or to be owned does now make or will make available to the low and moderate income groups a "Basic Checking or Other Transaction Account," such as follows:

1. Indicate the characteristics of accounts, including but not limited to:

   A. The number of check and deposit transactions allowed per month and the charges pertaining thereto.

   B. The varied periods of "Hold" placed upon accounts for deposited checks.

   C. The types and amounts of other charges imposed.

   D. The form(s) of identification required to open and use such accounts.

2. Briefly, identify the method by which the availability of such accounts is made known to the public.

IN CONSIDERATION OF THE STATISTICAL DATA REQUESTED UNDER ATTACHMENTS IV, V AND VI, DESCRIBE IN NARRATIVE FORM HOW EACH PENNSYLVANIA INSTITUTION INVOLVED IN THIS TRANSACTION RELATES TO THE ACTUAL CURRENT MARKET CONDITIONS EXISTENT IN THE RESPECTIVE AREAS NOW SERVED OR TO BE SERVED.

NOTICE OF FILING

APPLICATION FOR AN

INTERSTATE ACQUISITION

_____, of _____,
       (Corporate Title)   (City)

_____, and registered therein as a Bank Holding Company duly formed
  (State)
under the provisions of the Bank Holding Company Act of 1956 (12 USC 1841 et seq.; 70 Stat. 133, Public Law 84-511), hereby gives public notice of having filed with the Secretary of Banking of the Commonwealth of Pennsylvania, pursuant to the provisions of Section 116 of the Pennsylvania Banking Code of 1965, as amended, an application for approval by the Department of Banking to (DESIGNATE HEREAFTER THE NATURE OF THE PROPOSED TRANSACTION REGARDING THE ENTITY(S) BELOW).

_____
      (Corporate Title)

of _____
    (City)   (State)

and so, indirectly acquire:

_____
      (Corporate Title)

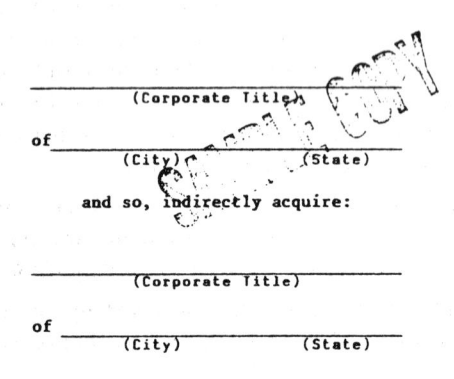

of _____
    (City)   (State)

Interested persons may express their views in writing regarding this proposal by submitting such to the Department of Banking. Such views may include, but are not limited to, comment on whether consummation of the proposal can reasonably be expected to produce and/or retain benefits to the public, such as greater convenience, increased competition, or gains in efficiency or employment, that outweigh possible adverse effects, such as undue concentration of resources, decreased or unfair competition or employment, conflicts of interests, or unsound banking practices. Any request for a hearing on this question must be accompanied by a statement of the reasons a written presentation would not suffice in lieu of a hearing, identifying specifically any questions of fact that are in dispute, summarizing the evidence that would be presented at a hearing, and indicating how the party commenting would be aggrieved by approval of the proposal.

Unless otherwise noted, comments regarding this application must be received at the Commonwealth of Pennsylvania, Department of Banking, 333 Market Street, Harrisburg, Pennsylvania 17101-2290, not later than fifteen (15) calendar days after the publication date of this notice.

EXHIBIT "H"

SAVINGS AND LOAN HOLDING COMPANY ACT
SECTION 408 OF THE NATIONAL HOUSING ACT OF 1934
12 U.S.C. § 1730a

(a) *Definitions.*

(1) As used in this section, unless the context otherwise requires—

(A) "insured institution" means a Federal savings and loan association, a Federal savings bank, a building and loan, savings and loan or homestead association or a cooperative bank, the accounts of which are insured by the Federal Savings and Loan Insurance Corporation, and shall include a Federal savings bank the deposits of which are insured by the Federal Deposit Insurance Corporation;

(B) "uninsured institution" means any association or bank referred to in subparagraph (A), the accounts of which are not insured by the Federal Savings and Loan Insurance Corporation, except for a Federal savings bank the deposits of which are insured by the Federal Deposit Insurance Corporation;

(C) "company" means any corporation, partnership, trust, joint-stock company, or similar organization, but does not include the Federal Savings and Loan Insurance Corporation, any Federal home loan bank, or any company the majority of the shares of which is owned by the United States or any State, or by an officer of the United States or any State in his official capacity, or by any instrumentality of the United States or any State;

(D) "savings and loan holding company" means any company which directly or indirectly controls an insured institution or controls any other company which is a savings and loan holding company by virtue of this subsection;

(E) "multiple savings and loan holding company" means any savings and loan holding company which directly or indirectly controls two or more insured institutions;

(F) "diversified savings and loan holding company" means any savings and loan holding company whose subsidiary insured institution and related activities as permitted under paragraph (2) of subsection (c) of this section represented, on either an actual or a pro forma basis, less than 50 per centum of its consolidated net worth at the close of its preceding fiscal year and of its consolidated net earnings for such fiscal year (or, during the first year's operation of the section, at such time as the holding company so qualifies), as determined in accordance with regulations issued by the Corporation;

(G) "person" means an individual or company;

(H) "subsidiary" of a person means any company which is controlled by such person, or by a company which is a subsidiary of such person by virtue of this subsection;

(I) "affiliate" of a specified insured institution means any person or company which controls, is controlled by, or is under common control with, such insured institution; and

(J) "State" includes the District of Columbia and the Commonwealth of Puerto Rico.

(2) For purposes of this section, a person shall be deemed to have control of—

(A) An insured institution if the person directly or indirectly or acting in concert with one or more other persons, or through one or more subsidiaries, owns, controls, or holds with power to vote, or holds proxies representing, more than 25 per centum of the voting shares of such insured institution, or controls in any manner the election of a majority of the directors of such institution;

(B) any other company if the person directly or indirectly or acting in concert with one or more other persons, or through one or more subsidiaries, owns, controls, or holds with power to vote, or holds proxies representing, more than 25 per centum of the voting shares or rights of such other company, or controls in any manner the election or appointment of a majority of the directors or trustees of such other company, or is a general partner in or has contributed more than 25 per centum of the capital of such other company;

(C) a trust if the person is a trustee thereof; or

(D) an insured institution or any other company if the Corporation determines, after reasonable notice and opportunity for hearing, that such person directly or indirectly exercises a controlling influence over the management or policies of such institution or other company.

(3) Notwithstanding any other provision of this subsection, the term "savings and loan holding company" does not include—

(A) any company by virtue of its ownership or control of voting shares of an insured institution or savings and loan holding company acquired in connection with the underwriting of securities if such shares are held only for such period of time (not exceeding one hundred and twenty days unless extended by the Corporation) as will permit the sale thereof on a reasonable basis; and

(B) any trust (other than a pension, profit-sharing, shareholders', voting, or business trust) which controls an insured institution or a savings and loan holding company if such trust by its terms must terminate within twenty-five years or not later than twenty-one years and ten months after the death of individuals living on the effective date of the trust, and is (i) in existence on June 26, 1967, or (ii) a testamentary trust created on or after June 26, 1967.

(b) *Registration and examination.*

(1) Within one hundred and eighty days after the enactment of the Savings and Loan Holding Company Amendments of 1967, or within ninety days after becoming a savings and loan holding company, whichever is later, each savings and loan holding company shall register with the Corporation on forms prescribed by the Corporation, which shall include such information, under oath or otherwise, with respect to the financial condition, ownership, operations, management, and intercompany relationships of such holding company and its subsidiaries, and related matters, as the Corporation may deem necessary or appropriate to carry out the

purposes of this section. Upon application, the Corporation may extend the time within which a savings and loan holding company shall register and file the requisite information.

(2) Each savings and loan holding company and each subsidiary thereof, other than an insured institution, shall file with the Corporation, the Federal home loan bank of the district in which its principal office is located, such reports as may be required by the Corporation. Such reports shall be made under oath or otherwise, and shall be in such form and for such periods, as the Corporation may prescribe. Each report shall contain such information concerning the operations of such savings and loan holding company and its subsidiaries as the Corporation may require.

(3) Each savings and loan holding company shall maintain such books and records as may be prescribed by the Corporation.

(4) Each savings and loan holding company and each subsidiary thereof shall be subject to such examinations as the Corporation may prescribe. The cost of such examinations shall be assessed against and paid by such holding company. Examination and other reports may be furnished by the Corporation to the appropriate State supervisory authority. The Corporation shall, to the extent deemed feasible, use for the purposes of this subsection reports filed with or examinations made by other Federal agencies or the appropriate State supervisory authority.

(5) The Corporation shall have power to require any savings and loan holding company, or persons connected therewith if it is not a corporation, to execute and file a prescribed form of irrevocable appointment of agent for service of process.

(6) The Corporation may at any time, upon its own motion or upon application, release a registered savings and loan holding company from any registration theretofore made by such company, if the Corporation shall determine that such company no longer has control of any insured institution.

(c) *Holding company activity.* Except as otherwise provided in this subsection—

(1) no savings and loan holding company or subsidiary thereof which is not an insured institution shall, for or on behalf of a subsidiary insured institution, engage in any activity or render any services for the purpose or with the effect of evading law or regulation applicable to such insured institution; and

(2) no multiple savings and loan holding company or subsidiary thereof which is not an insured institution shall commence, or continue for more than five years after the enactment of this amendment or for more than one hundred and eighty days after becoming a savings and loan holding company or subsidiary thereof (whichever is later), any business activity other than (A) furnishing or performing management services for a subsidiary insured institution, (B) conducting an insurance agency or an escrow business, (C) holding or managing or liquidating assets owned by or acquired from a subsidiary insured institution, (D) holding or managing properties used or occupied by a subsidiary insured institution, (E) acting as trustee under deed of trust, or (F) furnishing or performing such other services or engaging in such other activities as the Corporation may approve or may prescribe by regulation as being

a proper incident to the operations of insured institutions and not detrimental to the interests of savings account holders therein. The Corporation may, upon a showing of good cause, extend such time from year to year, for an additional period not exceeding three years, if the Corporation finds such extension would not be detrimental to the public interest.

(d) *Prohibited transactions.* No savings and loan holding company's subsidiary insured institution shall—

(1) invest any of its funds in the stock, bonds, debentures, notes, or other obligations of any affiliate (other than a service corporation as authorized by law);

(2) accept the stock, bonds, debentures, notes, or other obligations of any affiliate as collateral security for any loan or extension of credit made by such institution;

(3) purchase securities or other assets or obligations under repurchase agreement from any affiliate;

(4) make any loan, discount, or extension of credit to (A) any affiliate, except in a transaction authorized by subparagraph (A) of paragraph (6) of this subsection, or (B) any third party on the security of any property acquired from any affiliate, or with knowledge that the proceeds of any such loan, discount, or extension of credit, or any part thereof, are to be paid over to or utilized for the benefit of any affiliate: *Provided, however,* that with the prior written approval of the Corporation, a subsidiary insured institution may make a loan, discount, or extension of credit to a third party on the security of property acquired from a wholly owned affiliate service corporation. The Corporation shall grant approval of any application for approval under this subdivision if, in the opinion of the Corporation, such a loan, discount, or extension of credit would not be detrimental to the interests of savings account holders in the insured institution, or to the insurance risk of the Corporation with respect to such institution, and would not be a means of facilitating the sale of (1) property purchased from any savings and loan holding company or any affiliate thereof other than such service corporation, or (2) property heretofore owned, legally or beneficially, by any savings and loan holding company or affiliate thereof;

(5) guarantee the repayment of or maintain any compensating balance for any loan or extension of credit granted to any affiliate by any third party;

(6) except with the prior written approval of the Corporation—

(A) engage in any transaction with any affiliate involving the purchase, sale, or lease of property or assets (other than participating interests in mortgage loans to the extent authorized by regulations of the Corporation) in any case where the amount of the consideration involved when added to the aggregate amount of the consideration given or received by such institution for all such transactions during the preceding twelve-month period exceeds the lesser of $100,000 or 0.1 per centum of the institution's total assets at the end of the preceding fiscal year; or

(B) enter into any agreement or understanding, either in writing or orally, with any affiliate under which such affiliate is to (i) render management or advertising services for the institution, (ii) serve as a consultant, adviser, or agent for any phase of the operations of the institution, or (iii) render services of any other nature for the institution, other than those which may be exempted by regulation or order of the Corporation, unless the aggregate amount of the consideration required to be paid by such institution in the future under all such existing agreements or understandings cannot exceed the lesser of $100,000 or 0.1 per centum of the institution's total assets at the end of the preceding fiscal year; or

(C) make any payment to any affiliate under any agreement or understanding hereinabove referred to in subparagraph (B) where the institution has previously paid to affiliates during the preceding twelve-month period, pursuant to any such agreements or understandings, an amount aggregating in excess of the lesser of $100,000 or 0.1 per centum of the institution's total assets at the end of the preceding fiscal year.

The Corporation shall grant approval under this paragraph (6) if, in the opinion of the Corporation, the terms of any such transaction, agreement, or understanding, or any such payment by such institution, would not be detrimental to the interests of its savings account holders or to the insurance risk of the Corporation with respect to such institution.

(e) *Acquisitions*.

(1) It shall be unlawful for—

(A) any savings and loan holding company directly or indirectly, or through one or more subsidiaries or through one or more transactions—

(i) to acquire, except with the prior written approval of the Corporation, the control of an insured institution or a savings and loan holding company, or to retain the control of such an institution or holding company acquired or retained in violation of this section as heretofore or hereafter in effect;

(ii) to acquire, except with the prior written approval of the Corporation, by the process of merger, consolidation, or purchase of assets, another insured or uninsured institution or a savings and loan holding company, or all or substantially all of the assets of any such institution or holding company;

(iii) to acquire by purchase or otherwise, or to retain for more than one year after the enactment of this amendment, any of the voting shares of an insured institution not a subsidiary, or of a savings and loan holding company not a subsidiary, or, in the case of a multiple savings and loan holding company, to so acquire or retain more than 5 per centum of the voting shares of any company not a subsidiary which is engaged in any business activity other than those specified in paragraph (2) of subsection (c) of this section; or

(iv) to acquire the control of an uninsured institution, or to retain for more than one year after February 14, 1968, or from the date on which such control was acquired, whichever is later, [the control of any such institution] except that the Corporation may upon application by such company extend such one-year period from year to year, for an additional period not exceed three years, if the Corporation finds such extension is warranted and shall not be detrimental to the public interest;

(B) any other company, without the prior written approval of the Corporation, directly or indirectly, or through one or more subsidiaries or through one or more transactions, to acquire the control of one or more insured institutions, except that such approval shall not be required in connection with the control of an insured institution (i) acquired by devise under the terms of a will creating a trust which is excluded from the definition of "savings and loan holding company" under subsection (a) of this section, or (ii) acquired in connection with a reorganization in which a person or group of persons, having had control of an insured institution for more than three years, vests control of that institution in a newly formed holding company subject to the control of the same person or group of persons. The Corporation shall approve an acquisition of an insured institution under this subparagraph unless it finds the financial and managerial resources and future prospects of the company and institution involved to be such that the acquisition would be detrimental to the institution or the insurance risk of the Corporation, and shall render its decision within ninety days after submission to the Board of the complete record on the application.

[*Editor's Note:* Braketed language in the following paragraph 1730a(e)(2) will be removed, effective October 13, 1986.]

(2) The Corporation shall not approve any acquisition under subparagraphs (A)(i) or (A)(ii), or of more than one insured institution under subparagraph (B), of paragraph (1) of this subsection, [except a transaction under subsection (m) of this section] except in accordance with this paragraph. In every case, the Corporation shall take into consideration the financial and managerial resources and future prospects of the company and institution involved, and the convenience and needs of the community to be served, and shall render its decision within ninety days after submission to the Board of the complete record on the application. Before approving any such acquisition, [except a transaction under subsection (m) of this section] the Corporation shall request from the Attorney General and consider any report rendered within thirty days on the competitive factors involved. The Corporation shall not approve any proposed acquisition—

(A) which would result in a monopoly, or which would be in furtherance of any combination or conspiracy to monopolize or to attempt to monopolize the savings and loan business in any part of the United States, or

(B) the effect of which in any section of the country may be substantially to lessen competition, or tend to create a monopoly, on which any other manner would be in restraint of trade, unless it finds that the anticompetitive effects of the proposed acquisition are clearly outweighed in the public interest by the probable effect of the acquisition in meeting the convenience and needs of the community to be served.

(3) No acquisition shall be approved by the Corporation under this subsection which will—

(A) result in the formation by any company, through one or more subsidiaries or through one or more transactions, of a multiple savings and loan holding company controlling insured institutions in more than one state; or

(B) enable an existing multiple savings and loan holding company to acquire an insured institution the principal office of which is located in a State other than the State which such savings and loan holding company shall designate, by writing filed with the Corporation within sixty days after its registration hereunder, as the State in which the principal savings and loan business of such holding company is conducted.

(4) The provisions of this subsection and of subsections (c)(2) and (g) of this section shall not apply to any savings and loan holding company which acquired the control of an insured institution or of a savings and loan holding company pursuant to a pledge or hypothecation to secure a loan, or in connection with the liquidation of a loan, made in the ordinary course of business, but it shall be unlawful for any such company to retain such control for more than one year after the enactment of this amendment or from the date on which such control was acquired, whichever is later, except that the Corporation may upon application by such company extend such one-year period from year to year, for an additional period not exceeding three years, if the Corporation finds such extension is warranted and would not be detrimental to the public interest.

(f) *Declaration of dividends.* Every subsidiary insured institution of a savings and loan holding company shall give the Corporation not less than thirty days' advance notice of the proposed declaration by its directors of any dividend on its guaranty, permanent, or other nonwithdrawable stock. Such notice period shall commence to run from the date of receipt of such notice by the Corporation. Any such dividend declared within such period, or without the giving of such notice to the Corporation, shall be invalid and shall confer no rights or benefits upon the holder of any such stock.

(g) *Holding Company indebtedness.*

(1) No savings and loan holding company or any subsidiary thereof which is not an insured institution shall issue, sell, renew, or guarantee any debt security of such company or subsidiary, or assume any debt, without the prior written approval of the Corporation.

(2) The provisions of paragraph (1) of this subsection shall not apply to—

(A) a diversified savings and loan holding company or any subsidiary thereof; or

(B) the issuance, sale, renewal, or guaranty of any debt security, or the assumption of any debt, by any other savings and loan holding company or any subsidiary thereof, if such security or debt aggregates, together with all such other securities or debt then outstanding as to which such holding company or subsidiary is primarily or contingently liable, not more than 15 per centum of the consolidated net worth of such holding company or subsidiary at the end of the preceding fiscal year.

(3) The Corporation shall, upon application, approve any act or transaction not exempted from the application of paragraph (1) of this subsection if the Corporation finds that—

(A) the proceeds of any such act or transaction will be used for (i) the purchase of permanent, guaranty, or other nonwithdrawable stock to be issued by a subsidiary insured institution, or (ii) the purpose of making a capital contribution to a subsidiary insured institution; or

(B) such act or transaction is required for the purpose of refunding, extending, exchanging, or discharging an outstanding debt security, or for other necessary or urgent corporate needs, and would not impose an unreasonable or imprudent financial burden on the applicant. The Corporation may also approve any application under this paragraph if it finds that the act or transaction would not be injurious to the operation of any subsidiary insured institution in the light of its financial condition and prospects.

Applications filed with the Corporation pursuant to this subsection shall be in such form and contain such information as the Corporation may prescribe.

(4) If a State authority or any other agency of the United States, having jurisdiction of any act or transaction within the scope of paragraph (1) of this subsection, shall inform the Corporation, upon request by the Corporation for an opinion or otherwise, that State or Federal laws applicable thereto have not been complied with, the Corporation shall not approve such act or transaction until and unless the Corporation is satisfied that such compliance has been effected.

(5) As used in this subsection, the term "debt security" includes any note, draft, bond, debenture, certificate of indebtedness, or any other instrument commonly used as evidence of indebtedness, or any contract or agreement, under the terms of which any party becomes, or may become primarily or contingently liable for the payment of money, either in the present or at a future date.

(6) (A) If the Corporation finds that a diversified savings and loan holding company does not meet the test prescribed in subparagraph (B) of this paragraph, such holding company or any subsidiary thereof may not accept, use, or receive the benefit of any dividend on stock from a subsidiary insured institution, and such institution may not declare or pay any dividend on its stock to such holding company or subsidiary, unless the Corporation fails to object, within thirty days of receipt of notification under subsection (f) of this section, to such dividend as being injurious to the insured institution in the light of its financial condition and prospects.

(B) The prohibition of subparagraph (A) of this paragraph shall not apply to a diversified savings and loan holding company or any subsidiary thereof if, excluding its subsidiary insured institution, its consolidated net income available for interest for its preceding fiscal year was twice its consolidated debt service requirements for the twelve-month period next succeeding such fiscal year, as determined in accordance with regulations issued by the Corporation.

(h) *Administration and enforcement.*

(1) The Corporation is authorized to issue such rules, regulations, and orders as it deems necessary or appropriate to enable it to administer and carry out the purposes of this section, and to require compliance therewith and prevent evasions thereof.

(2) The Corporation may make such investigations as it deems necessary or appropriate to determine whether the provisions of this section, and rules, regulations, and orders thereunder, are being and have been complied with by savings and loan holding companies and subsidiaries and affiliates thereof. For the purpose of any investigation under this section, the Corporation or its designated representatives shall have power to administer oaths and affirmations, to issue subpoenas and subpoenas duces tecum, to take evidence, and to require the production of any books, papers, correspondence, memorandums, or other records which may be relevant or material to inquiry. The attendance of witnesses and the production of any such records may be required from any place in any State or in any territory. The Corporation may apply to the United States district court for the judicial district or the United States court in any territory in which any witness or company subpoenaed resides or carries on business, for enforcement of any subpoena or subpoena duces tecum issued pursuant to this paragraph, and such courts shall have jurisdiction and power to order and require compliance therewith.

(3) (A) In the course of or in connection with any proceeding under subsection (a)(2)(D) or under subsection (h)(5) of this section, the Corporation or its designated representatives, including any person designated to conduct any hearing under said subsection, shall have power to administer oaths and affirmations, to take or cause to be taken depositions, and to issue, revoke, quash, or modify subpoenas and subpoenas duces tecum; and the Corporation is empowered to make rules and regulations with respect to any such proceedings. The attendance of witnesses and the production of documents provided for in this paragraph may be required from any place in any State or in any territory at any designated place where such proceeding is being conducted. Any party to such proceedings may apply to the United States District Court for the District of Columbia, or the United States district court for the judicial district or the United States court in any territory in which such proceeding is being conducted, or where the witness resides or carries on business, for enforcement of any subpoena or subpoena duces tecum issued pursuant to this paragraph, and such courts shall have jurisdiction, and power to order and require compliance therewith. Witnesses subpoenaed under this section shall be paid the same fees and mileage that are paid witnesses in the district courts of the United States.

(B) Any hearing provided for in subsection (a)(2)(D) or under subsection (h)(5) of this section shall be held in the Federal judicial district or in the territory in which the principal office of the institution or other company is located unless the party afforded the hearing consents to another place, and shall be conducted in accordance with the provisions of chapter 5 of Title 5 of the United States Code.

(4) Whenever it shall appear to the Corporation that any person is engaged or has engaged or is about to engage in any acts or practices which constitute or will

constitute a violation of the provisions of this section or of any rule regulation or order thereunder, the Corporation may in its discretion bring an action in the proper United States district court, or the United States court of any territory or other place subject to the jurisdiction of the United States, to enjoin such acts or practices, to enforce compliance with this section or any rule, regulation, or order thereunder, or to require the divestiture of any acquisition in violation of this section, or for any combination of the foregoing, and such courts shall have jurisdiction of such actions, and upon a proper showing an injunction, decree, restraining order, order of divestiture, or other appropriate order shall be granted without bond.

(5) (A) Notwithstanding any other provision of this section, the Corporation may, whenever it has reasonable cause to believe that the continuation by a savings and loan holding company of any activity or of ownership or control of any of its noninsured subsidiaries constitutes a serious risk to the financial safety, soundness, or stability of a savings and loan holding company's subsidiary insured institution and is inconsistent with the sound operation of an insured savings and loan institution or with the purposes of this section or with the Financial Institutions Supervisory Act, order the savings and loan holding company or any of its subsidiaries, after due notice and opportunity for hearing, to terminate such activities or to terminate (within one hundred and twenty days or such longer period as the Corporation directs in unusual circumstances) its ownership or control of any such noninsured subsidiary either by sale or by distribution of the shares of the subsidiary to the shareholders of the savings and loan holding company. Such distribution shall be pro rata with respect to all of the shareholders of the distributing savings and loan holding company, and the holding company shall not make any charge to its shareholders arising out of such a distribution.

(B) The Corporation may in its discretion apply to the United States district court within the jurisdiction of which the principal office of the company is located, for the enforcement of any effective and outstanding order issued under this section, and such court shall have jurisdiction and power to order and require compliance therewith, but except as provided in subsection (k), no court shall have jurisdiction to affect by injunction or otherwise the issuance or enforcement of any notice or order under this section, or to review, modify, suspend, terminate, or set aside any such notice or order.

(6) All expenses of the Federal Home Loan Bank Board or of the Corporation under this section shall be considered as nonadministrative expenses.

(i) *Prohibited acts.* It shall be unlawful for—

(1) any savings and loan holding company or subsidiary thereof, or any director, officer, employee, or person owning, controlling, or holding with power to vote, or holding proxies representing, more than 25 per centum of the voting shares, of such holding company or subsidiary, to hold, solicit, or exercise any proxies in respect of any voting rights in an insured institution which is a mutual institution;

(2) any director or officer of a savings and loan holding company, or any person owning, controlling, or holding with power to vote, or holding proxies representing more than 25 per centum of the voting shares of such holding company

(A), except with the prior approval of the Corporation, to serve at the same time as a director, officer, or employee of an insured institution or another savings and loan holding company, not a subsidiary of such holding company, or (B) to acquire control, or to retain control for more than two years after the enactment of this subsection, of any insured institution not a subsidiary of such holding company; or

(3) any individual, except with the prior approval of the Corporation, to serve or act as a director, officer, or trustee of, or become a partner in, any savings and loan holding company after having been convicted of any criminal offense involving dishonesty or breach of trust.

(j) *Penalties.*

(1) Any company which willfully violates any provision of this section, or any rule, regulation, or order thereunder, shall upon conviction be fined not more than $1,000 for each day during which the violation continues.

(2) Any individual who willfully violates or participates in a violation of any provision of this section, or any rule, regulation, or order thereunder, shall upon conviction be fined not more than $10,000 or imprisoned not more than one year, or both.

(3) Every director, officer, partner, trustee, agent, or employee of a savings and loan holding company shall be subject to the same penalties for false entries in any book, report, or statement of such savings and loan holding company as are applicable to officers, agents, and employees of an institution the accounts of which are insured by the Corporation for false entries in any books, reports, or statements of such institution under Section 1006 of Title 18 of the United States Code.

(4) (A) Any company which violates or any individual who participates in a violation of any provision of this section, or any regulation or order issued pursuant thereto, shall forfeit and pay a civil penalty of not more than $1,000 per day for each day during which such violation continues: *Provided,* that the Corporation may, in its discretion, compromise, modify, or remit any civil money penalty which is subject to imposition or has been imposed under authority of this subsection. The penalty may be assessed and collected by the Corporation by written notice. As used in the section, the term "violates" includes without any limitation any action (alone or with another or others) for or toward causing, bringing about, participating in, counseling, or aiding or abetting a violation.

(B) In determining the amount of the penalty the Corporation shall take into account the appropriateness of the penalty with respect to the size of financial resources and good faith of the company or person charged, the gravity of the violation, the history of previous violations, and such other matters as justice may require.

(C) The company or person assessed shall be afforded an opportunity for agency hearing, upon request made within ten days after issuance of the notice of assessment. In such hearing all issues shall be determined on the record pursuant to Section 554 of Title 5, United States Code. The agency determination shall be made by final order which may be reviewed only as provided in subparagraph (D). If no hearing is requested as herein provided, the assessment shall constitute a final and unappealable order.

(D) Any company or person against whom an order imposing a civil money penalty has been entered after agency hearing under this section may obtain review by the United States court of appeals for the circuit in which the home office of the company is located, or in the United States Court of Appeals for the District of Columbia Circuit, by filing a notice of appeal in such court within thirty days from the date of such order, and simultaneously sending a copy of such notice by registered or certified mail to the Corporation. The Corporation shall promptly certify and file in such court the record upon which the penalty was imposed, as provided in Section 2112 of Title 28, United States Code. The findings of the Corporation shall be set aside if found to be unsupported by substantial evidence as provided by Section 706(2)(E) of Title 5, United States Code.

(E) If any company or person fails to pay an assessment after it has become a final and unappealable order, or after the court of appeals has entered final judgment in favor of the agency, the Corporation shall refer the matter to the Attorney General, who shall recover the amount assessed by action in the appropriate United States district court. In such action the validity and appropriateness of the final order imposing the penalty shall not be subject to review.

(F) The Corporation shall promulgate regulations establishing procedures necessary to implement this paragraph.

(G) All penalties collected under authority of this paragraph shall be covered into the Treasury of the United States.

(k) *Judicial review.* Any party aggrieved by an order of the Corporation under this section may obtain a review of such order by filing in the court of appeals of the United States for the circuit in which the principal office of such party is located, or in the United States Court of Appeals for the District of Columbia Circuit, within thirty days after the date of service of such order, a written petition praying that the order of the Corporation be modified, terminated, or set aside. A copy of such petition shall be forthwith transmitted by the clerk of the court to the Corporation, and thereupon the Corporation shall file in the court the record in the proceeding, as provided in Section 2112 of Title 28 of the United States Code. Upon the filing of such petition, such court shall have jurisdiction, which upon the filing of the record shall be exclusive, to affirm, modify, terminate, or set aside, in whole or in part, the order of the Corporation. Review of such proceedings shall be had as provided in chapter 7 of Title 5 of the United States Code. The judgment and decree of the court shall be final, except that the same shall be subject to review by the Supreme Court upon certiorari as provided in Section 1254 of Title 28 of the United States Code.

(l) *Saving provision.* Nothing contained in this section, other than any transaction approved under subsection (e)(2) or (m), shall be interpreted or construed as approving any act, action, or conduct which is or has been or may be in violation of existing law, nor shall anything herein contained constitute a defense to any action, suit, or proceeding pending or hereafter instituted on account of any act, action, or conduct in violation of the antitrust laws.

[*Editor's Note:* The following subsection (m) expired on October 13, 1986.]

(m) [*Emergency thrift acquisitions.*]

(1)(A)(i) Notwithstanding any provisions of the laws or constitution of any State or any provision of Federal law, except as provided in subsections (e)(2) and (1) of this section, and in clause (iii) of this subparagraph, the Corporation, upon its determination that severe financial conditions exist which threaten the stability of a significant number of insured institutions, or of insured institutions possessing significant financial resources, may authorize, in its discretion and where it determines such authorization would lessen the risk to the Corporation, an insured institution that is eligible for assistance pursuant to Section 406(f) of this Act to merge or consolidate with, or to transfer its assets and liabilities to, any other insured institution or any insured bank (as such term "insured bank" is defined in Section 3(h) of the Federal Deposit Insurance Act), may authorize any other insured institution to acquire control of said insured institution, or may authorize any company to acquire control of said insured institution or to acquire the assets or assume the liabilities thereof.

(ii) Mergers, consolidations, transfers, and acquisitions under this subsection shall be on such terms as the Corporation shall provide.

(iii) Where otherwise required by law, transactions under this subsection must be approved by the primary Federal supervisor of the party thereto that is not an insured institution.

(B)(i) Before making a determination to take any action under subparagraph (A), the Corporation shall consult the State official having jurisdiction of the acquired institution.

(ii) The State official shall be given a reasonable opportunity, and in no event less than forty-eight hours, to object to the use of the provisions of this paragraph. Such notice may be provided by the Corporation prior to its appointment as receiver, but in anticipation of an impending appointment.

(iii) If the State official objects during such period, the Corporation may use the authority of this paragraph only by a unanimous vote of the Federal Home Loan Bank Board. The Federal Home Loan Bank Board shall provide to the State official, as soon as practicable, a written certification of its determination.

(2) In considering authorizations under this subsection, the Corporation may solicit such offers or proposals as are practicable from any prospective purchasers or merger partners it determines, in its sole discretion, are both qualified and capable of acquiring the assets and liabilities of the insured institution.

(3)(A) If, after receiving offers, the offer presenting the lowest expense to the Corporation, that is in a form and with conditions acceptable to the Corporation (hereinafter referred to as the "lowest acceptable offer") is from an institution that is not an existing in-State insured institution or an in-State savings and loan holding company, the Corporation shall permit each offeror who made an offer the estimated cost of which to the Corporation was within 15 per centum or $15,000,000, whichever is less, of the initial lowest acceptable offer to submit a new offer.

(B) In considering authorizations under this subsection, the Corporation shall give consideration to the need to minimize the cost of financial assistance and to the maintenance of specialized depository institutions. The Corporation shall authorize transactions under this subsection considering the following priorities:

(i) First, between depository institutions of the same type within the same State;

(ii) Second, between depository institutions of the same type in different States;

(iii) Third, between depository institutions of different types in the same State; and

(iv) Fourth, between depository institutions of different types in different States.

(C) In the case of a minority-controlled institution, the Corporation shall seek an offer from other minority-controlled institutions before proceeding with the sequence set forth in the preceding subparagraph.

(D) In considering offers from different States, the Corporation shall give a priority to offers from adjoining States.

(E) In determining the cost of offers and reoffers under this subsection, the Corporation's calculations and estimations shall be determinative. The Corporation may set reasonable time limits on offers and reoffers.

(4) For purposes of this subsection—

(A) the term "insured depository institution" means an insured institution or a bank insured by the Federal Deposit Insurance Corporation; and

(B) the term "in-State depository institution or in-State depository institution holding company" means an existing insured depository institution currently operating in the State in which the closed institution is chartered or a company that is operating an insured depository institution subsidiary in the State in which the closed institution is chartered.

(5) (A) Where a merger, consolidation, transfer, or acquisition under this subsection involves an insured institution eligible for assistance and a bank or banking holding company, an insured institution may retain and operate any existing branch or branches or any other existing facilities but otherwise shall be subject to the conditions upon which a national bank may establish and operate branches in the State in which such insured institution is located.

(B) No such insured institution shall move its principal office or any branch office after it is acquired which it would be prohibited from moving if it were a national bank.

(C)(i) Notwithstanding the foregoing, if such an insured institution does not have its home office in the State of the bank holding company bank subsidiary, and if such institution does not qualify as a domestic building and loan association under Section 7701(a)(19) of the Internal Revenue Code of 1954, or does not meet the asset composition test imposed by subparagraph (C) of that section on institutions seeking so to qualify, then such insured institution shall be subject to the conditions upon which a bank may retain, operate, and establish branches in the State in which the insured institution is located.

(ii) The Corporation, for good cause shown, may allow insured institutions up to two years to comply with the requirements of clause (i).

(n) *Holding company activity of nonqualifying domestic building and loan association.* A savings and loan holding company, or any subsidiary thereof which is not an insured institution, whose subsidiary insured institution fails to qualify as a domestic building and loan association under Section 7701(a)(19) of the Internal Revenue Code of 1954, may not commence, or continue for more than three years after such failure, any business activity other than those specified for multiple savings and loan holding companies and their subsidiaries under subsection (c)(2) of this section.

NOTES

NOTES

NOTES